T0147655

atta girl

atta girl

Tales from a Life in the Trenches of Show Business

peggy pope

iUniverse, Inc.
Bloomington

atta girl
Tales from a Life in the Trenches of Show Business

Copyright © 2011 by peggy pope

All rights reserved. No part of this book may be used or reproduced by any means, graphic, electronic, or mechanical, including photocopying, recording, taping or by any information storage retrieval system without the written permission of the publisher except in the case of brief quotations embodied in critical articles and reviews.

iUniverse books may be ordered through booksellers or by contacting:

iUniverse
1663 Liberty Drive
Bloomington, IN 47403
www.iuniverse.com
1-800-Authors (1-800-288-4677)

Because of the dynamic nature of the Internet, any web addresses or links contained in this book may have changed since publication and may no longer be valid. The views expressed in this work are solely those of the author and do not necessarily reflect the views of the publisher, and the publisher hereby disclaims any responsibility for them.

ISBN: 978-1-4620-4098-8 (sc)
ISBN: 978-1-4620-4100-8 (hc)
ISBN: 978-1-4620-4099-5 (ebk)

Library of Congress Control Number: 2011913260

Printed in the United States of America

iUniverse rev. date: 11/02/2011

Front cover picture by David Rodgers
Back cover picture: "Nine to Five" (c) 1980 Twentieth Century Fox. All rights reserved

For
Alain Chuat of
Schweiz/Switzerland

who sent me two dollars for an autograph on September 29th, 2008
and thus reaffirmed for me that I was still marketable.

Contents

ACT III: CALIFORNIA

AFTERWORD

Introduction

Let Me Entertain You

About two weeks after *Nine to Five* opened, four young men in a convertible were passing the Egyptian movie theater on Hollywood Boulevard, where the stars leave their hand—and footprints on the sidewalk. I was on the sidewalk, too, my Rent-A-Wreck car having broken down again. When the boys saw me, they started screaming: "*Nine to Five! Nine to Five!* Loved you in *Nine to Five!* Seen it seventeen times!"

I was startled, not knowing how to respond and wondering if they might give me a lift, but then thinking better of that. They might ask me for money. They might be on drugs. Jane Fonda was still getting death threat letters twelve years after Vietnam, and I'd been in the movie with her. They might add me to their hit list. I wished they'd go away, but when they did, I felt lonely. *What is that all about?*

I once saw Dustin Hoffman on a talk show, and he told how he hated being recognized and hassled by fans but said that if he walked down the street and they didn't recognize him, he'd begin to worry about his career slipping. So he'd go stand in front of Bloomingdale's until somebody would say, "Oh, look, Dustin Hoffman! *The Graduate!*"

The fellows in the convertible weren't kidding. The movie *Nine to Five* was a cult film. When the video came out, people rented it, invited their friends over, and said all the lines together while they watched it. Twenty-seven years later, they're still at it.

It was a hit, globally, and through the miracle of dubbing, I became an instant linguist in French, Italian, Spanish, Russian, German, Japanese, Greek, Hungarian, Portuguese, Swedish, and Urdu. It was one of the highest-grossing pictures of the eighties. There was an immediate identification with this film based on the true stories of sexual harassment and the indignities suffered by secretaries in the seventies, before they found out could sue the bastards. Possibly 90 percent of the urban population works in an office or has done so at one time. Casting Dolly Parton, Jane Fonda, and Lily Tomlin as secretaries, ludicrous as that may seem, was brilliant. How could it not be a hit?

I almost didn't get into the film. I'd read about it and tried to get an interview for it, as there had to be a lot of parts for women playing secretaries. I called and wrote, but no, they weren't going to see me—"No," "Not interested," "Wrong time," "No, no, no," "All cast," "Forget it." It got through to me that I wasn't wanted, and that was that.

The weekend before filming started, my agent called and said, "Would you like to go in on *Nine to Five?* They want to see you."

They? I thought. *Who are "they"? They who have decided to control my life.* The script came, and when I looked at it, I saw that mine was yet another very small part.

For twenty years before going to California, I had been doing leads in plays. Hollywood was a place where, if you got a part saying two or three lines along with a close-up, it could overshadow all the leading parts in all the plays you'd ever done. Everybody would know you the next day. That's why I was in this godforsaken town. It's called building a career.

With this in mind, I went to the interview with a kind of exhausted indifference. It was just another couple of lines to me. As I waited to see the director, a woman with white hair came in, and I thought, *Oh, I see. That's probably who they want.* Then someone said, "Peggy Pope, will you come in, please?" I went into the cramped office and sat down at a small desk across from Colin Higgins, the writer and director. After some pleasantries, he said, "Actually, I had a somewhat older woman in mind." I said, perhaps a little too brusquely, "Oh, well, if you want old, there's old sitting out in the waiting room. Why don't you get her?"

He straightened up in his chair. It was like I had swatted him.

He said, "You know, I've never heard an actress talk that way." He paused and said, "Since I wrote this script, I could, with a flick of my pen, make her younger."

He seemed to be asking my advice, so in my new position as co-writer, I said thoughtfully, "Yeah, you could do that."

He said, "Could you, ah . . . would you mind reading a little of this for me?

Having spent eighty bucks on a coach to work on the part with me the day before, I said, "Sure, of course.

Colin Higgins, God bless him, gave me a leg up that day with a flick of his pen, casting me as the office lush secretly sipping away from a little flask kept in the file drawer. Every time Dolly, Lily, or Jane stormed out of the boss's office in a righteous rage, it was up to me to cheer her on with an "Atta girl!" I was a sort of boozy Greek chorus.

It was a good movie and a good part; at the end, my character comes back from rehab, hair combed, looking spiffy, and ready for the sequel. Under-dogs climbing to the top is a fine formula, and it's always good to be in at the end of a film so that people remember you were in it.

Prologue

I lived through my mother saying more than once, that she would "no more do that than go to the moon" and my father announcing just as often, that he was "going down to the cellar to shake up the furnace."

I lived through times way before free love, *Roe v. Wade*, condoms, and AIDS. Hell, I spent twenty-five years as a virgin so a man would respect me and propose. "A kiss was a promise" in those days. If a girl got pregnant with no husband to show for it, she'd have to find someone who'd put her in touch with the "Angel of Ashford" instead. That was a doctor in Pennsylvania who wore a half-inch-long fetus curled up in a bracelet on his wrist. Or maybe she'd go to Puerto Rico, where she could get an abortion that didn't entail the use of a clothes hanger. However she dealt with it, it was first-degree murder if she got caught.

The gangster, Dutch Schultz, was brought to justice—shot and killed—three towns away from ours. I can still see the oversize headlines in the *Newark Evening News,* folded and tossed with deadly aim onto our doorstep by a boy on a bike, causing a hullabaloo as all four of us children tore into it and fought to get to the comics that we loved: *Dick Tracy, Major Hoople, Blondie, The Katzenjammer Kids, Li'l Abner.*

My grandfather worked on the building of the railroads in the Southwest and once did a man a favor there. This man told my grandfather that he'd give him whatever he wanted in return. My grandfather said, "I want a seat on the stock exchange," the price of which was $25,000 at the time. The man gave it to him, but we never learned what the favor had been. Soon, Grandpa was playing poker with Diamond Jim Brady and Lillian Russell and was worth $7 million—before the crash in 1929. After that, his fortune vanished, and he lived in a rented room in Queens with his caretaker, Mrs. Merrill.

There was Lucky Lindy flying solo across the Atlantic, to my mother's astonishment, although it didn't stop her from saying, "I would no more do that than go to the moon." Then the Lindbergh baby was kidnapped. Later, Amelia Earhart, whose name I had carved into the beech tree as tall as our house, disappeared over the Pacific.

On *The March of Time* newsreel, we saw the Hindenburg, a hydrogen-filled dirigible, explode in the air and sink in slow motion as flames consumed its passengers and crew. Later, on the radio in my parents' bedroom, Orson Welles announced that aliens had landed in New Jersey, and we couldn't get the operator on the telephone. I didn't know what *aliens* meant and nobody would tell me, so I went down into the cellar and gave my dog, Molly, a bath in case they dropped by.

Isadora Duncan's scarf got caught in the spokes of the wheel of her escort's car and strangled her. I didn't understand why anyone would wear such a long scarf around her neck. It seemed to me to be asking for it. Anita Zahn, her disciple, taught us creative dancing on the lawn of the Women's Club of Upper Montclair, the same place where we gave a recital during which my slipper flew off my foot and sailed high in the air to dangle from the branch of a tree while the grown-ups laughed.

My brother Jim warned me to beware of old ladies with white hair who would stop in their limousines and offer a ride. "Never get in," he told me. "She'll stick you with a long hat pin full of drugs, and you'll be whisked off to South America and end up in the white-slave trade."

The summer ended. I was about to go to school for the first time! The world was opening up. My sister Adeline, as in "Sweet Adeline," would take me there. She was in sixth grade, and I would be in kindergarten. The school was two lots away from our house, just cut up the back, through the Kelloggs' cornfield, and past the Gilbreths', where the children lined up for the bathroom according to the efficiency schedule posted on the refrigerator. (Later, there would be a book called *Cheaper by the Dozen* and three movies about them as well.) Then we would turn left on High Street, and there it was: Nishuane Public School. Over one door, it said, "Boys"; over another was carved "Girls."

Nishuane included kids from kindergarten through sixth grade, and it demanded good marks from its students. Some schools pushed everyone on to seventh grade in another school, but not Nishuane. If you flunked a year, you could repeat it until you passed. The girls always passed, but some of the boys didn't. They were only interested in playing football and couldn't care less what grade they were in. They would grow tall over the summer. One was close to six feet that year. When a boy got to be six feet, regardless of what grade he was in, he was asked to leave and go find a job.

On the afternoon before the first day of school, Adeline—Sweet Adeline—came home and said to my mom, "Mother, what does *fuck* mean?" Mom said, "Where did you hear that word?" And Adeline said, "At the playground at school. One of the big boys asked me if I wanted to."

The next day, as the autumn sun glinted down on us, we were enrolled in the Kimberley Day School for Girls. Life had sent me spinning into a safe deposit box for the subsequent sixteen years.

Act I: Beginnings

Mom

My mother was born in 1886, the year Coca-Cola was invented, in the horse-and-buggy days. The railroads were still being built across the country. The slaves had only recently been freed. Women remained tethered to the home, where they raised many children and weren't allowed to vote. Only a few of them escaped to pursue careers. When my mother had gentlemen callers, my grandfather went to the stair landing at ten p.m. and set off an alarm clock to advise the young men that it was time for them to leave.

My mother and father met at a Halloween party, where they were both dressed as ghosts in white sheets. They stood together over the hot air heater in the floor, talking, while the sheets billowed around them. They courted for four years and were engaged for four more.

Grandpa Muir had misgivings about Dad; he thought he was a bit of a playboy and had too much fun. When Dad finished his residency at the New York Eye and Ear hospital, Grandpa asked him which he would prefer as a wedding present, a trip to Europe or a house in New Rochelle. Dad saw through the trick question and said, "A house in New Rochelle, of course, sir." Grandpa gave up trying to keep his favorite daughter home with him and offered them his blessing.

My mother told me that on their wedding night, my dad waited patiently while she knelt beside the bed and said her prayers.

When it was my turn to be born, my mom was forty-three my dad was fifty. My dad was so delighted with his prowess that he concocted a theatre piece for the event. He set up a trap to catch me in case no one was home when the stork arrived. I might wander over to the Kelloggs when it left. The trap was disguised as a rose trellis. I have a photo of my brothers, Jim and Bruce, standing beside this trellis trap, with my five year old sister, Adeline, standing in for me, posed on one leg in an arabesque, tangled up among the roses, captured. I spent a lot of time later on with the family album, pondering that event. It had the look of Edward Gorey about it. It was a hard copy of my parents' imagination, odd, romantic, and screwed up. I fit right in.

Dad

My father was the star of our family, the mover, the shaker, the man who told us what to do and how to do it. If we didn't shape up—for instance, if we came home with a B instead of an A on our report cards—he would mock us jauntily in song:

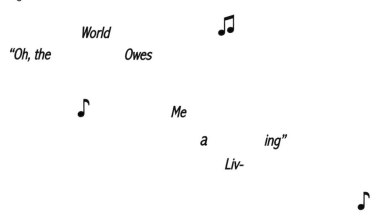

He had a two-part philosophy of life.

1. The world is out to get you; it's dog-eat-dog out there."
2. You'd better be first if you want to make the grade."

After reminding us of these principles, he'd go into his closet and take a slug of bourbon from a hip flask he kept there.

Franklin Roosevelt infuriated him: "Makes my blood boil." Socialized medicine was socialized bossism: "Nobody's going to tell me how to treat my patients." The WPA, FDR's answer to unemployment during the Depression, was, in his opinion, a bunch of freeloaders who stood around leaning on their shovels looking for a handout.

I spent a great deal of time staring out our front window at a ditch digger leaning on his shovel. One day the shovel's handle broke in two, throwing him to the ground. When I told my father about it that night, he studied me, his eyes hard with righteousness, and said, "See?" I wanted him to be clearer, but he was inside his thoughts and I didn't seem to be there anymore.

One Halloween when some children came to the front door and held out their paper sacks, he invited them into the hallway, where he had just put down his medical bag and hung up his coat. He said, "C'mon in here. Make yourselves at home," and led them into the living room.

"Now, what are you going to do for us?" my father asked them.

They turned and looked at each other, their large eyes filling with suspicion. My father enlightened them.

"Before we can give you anything, you must do something for us."

They looked at him blankly. One child giggled. The smallest one burst into tears, which soon developed into a wail.

I was writhing with embarrassment for them, for my father, for myself as a partner in this surprise entrapment of our small neighbors.

"You could sing a song," he went on, "or do a dance or tell us a story. Then we can give you some candy and treats. That's the meaning of Halloween, don'cha know?"

Each child was tricked into telling us something or doing a little dance. One of them even whistled "Dixie." After all had participated, they were each given a treat for their efforts. Into the paper bag it went, and then they were out of there, in an altered state of consciousness. I was awed by their performances. It was a first for me. I wondered how they had learned to entertain us so fast. My father found the whole evening a great success.

Jimmy Durante

When Jimmy Durante was starting out, still an unknown, singing and playing at a piano bar in Coney Island, he needed to see an ear, nose, and throat doctor. That doctor turned out to be my father the ear, nose, and throat specialist.

In those days, the doctor—specialist or not—personally took down all the information on the patient. It was a much more caring arrangement than we have today.

"And what do you do, Mr. Durante?" asked my father.

Jimmy, sounding like a Brooklyn construction worker with his rock-rough, gnarled voice, said, "I sing, Doc."

My dad didn't believe him, so Durante invited my parents to come hear him at the club. They went, and they were the only customers there. It didn't faze Jimmy at all. He changed the lyrics of *If I Had You* to *But I Have You.* He knew where he was going—to sing for huge audiences with a wall of romantic strings to back him up. He had autographed pictures ready to hand out and gave my parents several, for the whole family. He wrote a special one for Bruce, who was sick.

It was my first introduction to a celebrity, to a star, and I looked at that picture often as a child—the big nose; the huge, open smile; the light twinkling in his eyes; the pleasure glowing in his face. He seemed to invite me to join him, and I sensed that his world was different from mine and that I might prefer to live there. I listened to him faithfully on the radio. His voice was extraordinary; the musicality perfection; the communication complete. When he spoke of the sound he made, he said, "Them is the conditions that prevails." *My kind of guy,* I thought.

A few years later, after he had developed a reputation and some fame, he remained the same, sounding and looking like the cousin of a bum who might have slept outdoors the previous night. When he came around to my dad's hospital to visit a friend who was recuperating there, he was carrying flowers. The receptionist thought he was a delivery man and sent him around to the freight elevator, so he went up the back way. When the nurses upstairs told the receptionist what she had done, she was horrified. But it didn't matter to Jimmy how he got upstairs.

Corn

In our dining room, Dad was having an argument with Nellie, the new cook. Her hair was gathered in a bun on top of her head and wisped down on the sides. They were arguing about the carving knife. "It's dirty," said my father. "No, it's not," said Nellie in a heightened Irish accent. "It's water stains. Here, give it to me." She wiped it on her apron and offered it back to him. This did not go over well with my father. He was a doctor and believed in germs. "For God's sake, Nellie! What the hell are you doing?" Nellie said, "It's clean now. You can see yourself in it." My father's face turned red and his voice rose. "That's no way to clean the silver! Damn it, what's the matter with you?" The dog barked, left her puppies, and ran in from the laundry room to defend him.

Nellie stood with her hands on her hips and said, "So that's the way you get mad, huh?"

The dog stopped barking and ran back to her puppies. My father clenched his jaw, gripped the arms of his chair, looked straight ahead at the centerpiece of roses from the garden, and said, "Just go and get me a clean knife."

Nellie came back from the kitchen, handed my father a fresh knife, raised her eyebrows, pinched her lips together, and made a stout-hearted exit.

My brothers exchanged a look. My mother said, "Jim, will you start the mint jelly around the table, please?" My sister reached for her water glass, misjudged the distance, and knocked it over. "Oh, Adeline," my brothers groaned, their voices dripping with disdain. I'm ashamed to say I echoed them. She was so vulnerable. She invited our cruelty, and we were merciless. Napkins were passed to her while my father carved the lamb. Grandmother Pope looked on from her portrait above the fireplace, holding a fan in her lap and wearing an onyx and gold ring. The white skin of her face, forearms, and neck stood out against a black taffeta dress trimmed in lace. The armchair she sat in blended into a dark background, and she never took her eyes off of me. I dropped my napkin so that I would have to go under the table to retrieve it; she couldn't see me there, but when I came back, she was still sizing me up.

When the lamb, the vegetables, and the mint jelly had been passed around, I seized the opportunity to collect for the manners pot.

"Elbows on the table! Ten cents!" I had caught my brother Jim, and he had to put ten cents in the pot. The fine was usually a nickel, but elbows were major. When the pot was filled up, it paid for a trip to the movies. *Strangers in the Night* with Merle Oberon was playing through that Saturday, and I really wanted to see it.

We were concentrating on eating corn on the cob with a fork that summer, so there was a good chance we would have a full pot of fines by the end of the meal. You had to put your fork horizontally along the rows of corn, twist, and lift. I could get only three or four kernels at a time.

"Three weeks, kids. Three weeks to get that corn from the cob to your mouth," said my dad. "Don't disgrace me now."

"Who is Mrs. Prentice?" I said.

"She's John D. Rockefeller's daughter. She's giving the hospital money, and we're going to her farm for lunch," said my mother.

"Only if we know how to eat corn on the cob with a fork when we get there," said Dad, as he jammed his fork alongside his corncob and ripped off a mouthful of kernels. Gradually, he transferred his feelings about Nellie to the corn. "See that? See that? It can be done! Come on. Don't let me down. Don't give up."

We dug in and collected more money for the manners pot as the conversation drifted over my head, with subjects like Farming for Famine, Roosevelt and Germany, and Grandpa Muir and Mrs. Merrill.

We had strawberries and Borden's heavy cream for desert. The manners pot filled up, and we went to see Myrna Loy, William Powell, and their dog, Asta, in *The Thin Man.*

Dinner at the Prentice farm three weeks later turned out favorably. We were invited back for Christmas even though Adeline dropped her peach melba, passed around by the butler, into the finger bowl with a splash, and when Mrs. Prentice told us that the china plates were set in gold, we picked them up and held them over our heads to inspect their bottoms.

We watched Mr. Prentice gnaw his way from left to right and back again on a corncob and then hold his napkin up in front of his face and pick his teeth with a gold toothpick. My father told funny stories at dinner but was curiously quiet on the drive home.

Betty Boop

In the pop-up book of my life, I find moments that jump out to hand me knowledge, *gratis*. I love that. A surge of energy thrills through me. It's like a life promotion.

The Junk Man delivered one of these moments to me. I loved the Junk Man. He'd come by in a wagon drawn by a bony old horse at 2:30 every afternoon. Cowbells, strung across the wagon, announced him, clanging to the rhythm of the clippety-clops. I counted on him. *Clang, clang, clippety-clop*. Half past two. I'd run across the front lawn to look at what was new.

He was old and had whiskers that started in his ears, grew all around the lower part of his face, and covered his neck. He looked like a retired Santa Claus who'd lost a lot of weight and didn't wash. He didn't say "Hello" or "How do you do?" or anything like that. He was from some other country and hardly spoke any English. He bought and sold stuff, all secondhand, used, broken stuff. He always had something new to sell or trade, some new old thing.

One day my parents had gone to the hospital to be with my brother, Bruce. He was having another operation Jim was away at college, and Adeline had shut herself up in her room and wouldn't play with me anymore. We had been wrestling, my favorite thing to do. I would make her get down on her knees so we'd be the same height and I could knock her over. But that day she had gotten up suddenly and said, "I have to go upstairs for a minute. I'll be right back."

She didn't come back. *And* she locked her door.

In a rage, I took my Betty Boop doll, my best friend, and swung her by her feet at Adeline's door, expecting the door to open on impact. But it was Betty Boop's head that cracked open instead, and I saw that she did not have supernatural powers after all. There were chips from her face all over the hall floor. And she'd lost one of her eyes as well. I was devastated.

Then I heard cowbells, and I ran down to the Junk Man and asked him what to do.

"Give me," he said.

I handed cracked-headed, half-blind Betty Boop to him. He looked at her, shook his head, looked at me, and said, "I got."

He leaned back in his wagon, pulled out a Raggedy Andy doll, and handed him to me.

"Take. Good trade."

It was the best trade we ever made—a Betty Boop doll with one eye missing for a Raggedy Andy with no trousers. A pop-up day.

When Bruce got well, I planned to show Raggedy Andy to him, make him laugh.

Dad and the Art of Archery

"Life is a sea filled with shipwrecks," Dad would say. "You need to know how to survive in this dog-eat-dog world. You gotta outwit the next guy. Be a step ahead."

That winter when I was six, I went downstairs to breakfast and saw my dad outside the kitchen window spraying the garden hose.

"Why is Daddy watering the snow?" I asked.

"He's making a skating pond for you to learn to skate on. Here's your orange juice," said my mother.

So after breakfast, wearing my two-tone-green ski suit and hat and my sister's cast-off double runners, there I was on my own private skating pond. My father placed a kitchen chair in front of me and said, "Face the chair, grab hold of the seat, and push! See, that way you won't fall down." I looked up at him through the spindles of the chair back, his white hair shining in the sun. I pushed the chair toward him.

"Good. Good. Keep pushing! That's it! That's how you learn to skate."

"Oh," I said.

He watched for a minute or two till he was satisfied I'd gotten the idea, and while I wasn't looking, he went off to the city to take out other people's children's tonsils.

My father was there until I was thirteen. There was a lot of him. He taught me many things. He taught me how to whittle a stick with a penknife and shoot a .410-gauge shotgun, as well as how to spin a lariat and hop in and out of the loop, like Will Rogers was doing on the stage in New York. We built a jitney to get around in and planted a vegetable garden. He paid me fifty cents a bushel for crabgrass correctly pulled, so it wouldn't grow back. "Thar's gold in them thar hills," he would say. Then he taught me how to win at badminton by slamming the shuttlecock straight down at my opponent's feet and at croquet by knocking my opponent's ball so far out of the court that there was no way he'd get back before I got to the end post. The day I was about to beat him at checkers on the DL&W. commuter train, he pretended the train had lurched, causing his knee to upend the board and send the checkers flying just as I was making the final move, so the game didn't count. I was disappointed. He took out the *New York World-Telegram* and turned to the editorials, which irritated him more than usual. Maybe I was mistaken. Maybe he didn't want me to win for some reason. But wasn't that the point? Wasn't he always telling us to go out there and win? I chose to see this as a lesson, too—one I would understand later on, perhaps.

Another day, he brought home a bow, some arrows, and a bull's-eye target, which he set up among the peonies in the backyard.

"Here, try this," he said. "Take a firm stance, legs apart."

He stood behind me, guiding me. I raised the bow and pulled back on the bowstring to sight along the arrow at the target.

"That's it. Now aim above the highest circle, take a half-breath, hold it, and let go the string."

Pfft—thwap! Bull's-eye. I heard the "oowuh, oowuh," of a mourning dove behind the garage.

"Son of a gun," said my father. Then he said, "Do it again. It's all right to breathe now."

A few arrows later, he was off doing other things that needed his attention around the property—the grass, the roses, the grill for the picnic next day. I was left alone to prepare for my role in this dog-eat-dog world.

It was a Saturday. I liked how the stillness of the afternoon was broken only by the zinging of my arrows and, once in a while, the cooing of the mourning dove. Doves usually sang only in the evening when I was trying to get to sleep or in the morning to wake me up when I didn't want to get out of bed and go to school.

I practiced for a while, and then I shot a tree. Then I shot right through an old tire hanging from the tree. I shot the head off a peony, a sock off the clothesline, my dog's water dish, a birdbath, the lawn mower, the wheelbarrow, a new invasion of crabgrass, the garage, and the house, just as my father was coming up out of the cellar.

To hit a moving target, you have to aim ahead of it. How far ahead hangs on how fast it's moving, how far away it is, how heavy your bow is, how fast the arrow flies, and how much your body moves while trying to hold still. And on the beat of your heart. I was hitting everything that day. I was a natural at this.

Pfft—thunk. My arrow shot right across the bridge of my father's nose and shivered in the wood of the open cellar door. My father stood as still as the afternoon. Then, in slow motion, he turned his head and looked at me. He looked at the bow and arrow, the target, the rose garden, and the lilac bush. Then he went up the porch steps and into the house.

I sat down where I had been standing on the hot crabgrass and waited for him to come back out and punish me. But he didn't. I listened to the dove practicing. I put the target away in the garage so it wouldn't get wet if it rained. I puttered around in there until I could get back into my body, which had gone numb. Finally, I went into the house to look for my father. I found him in the living room, asleep on the sofa with the dog asleep on top of him.

The Wind and the Thistle

With our toy closet full of discarded lethal weapons, my father moved on to the world of entertainment. Undaunted by the archery incident, he turned his concentration to our somewhat proficient ice skating. He got a family membership to the New York Figure Skating Club, which was just down the street from where he practiced medicine. He was raising money for the new Midtown Hospital, at which he was the executive surgeon, and was reaching out to people like the Prentices and other influential citizens of the city who might become supporters.

"This can lead to all sorts of opportunities," he said. "You know Newbold Morris is there every Thursday night? He's the president of the City Council of New York City. Right up there with LaGuardia. And Rod Stephens Jr.? Builds sailing ships? In the America's Cup race every year. There's a Miss Kasser in a mink coat, greets the children in the afternoon sessions. We'll be in the ice show they put on in the spring," he said as he drove us into the skating rink in the city.

The annual Club Carnival took place in the old Madison Square Garden. It was directed over a loudspeaker by Leon Leonidoff of Radio City Music Hall and Rockettes fame. He singled me out at one point and gave me my first direction: While delivering notes to a group at the other end of the arena, he suddenly boomed out, "Will the little girl in the pink tutu at the Forty-Ninth Street side of the rink please stop spinning?"

My part in the show was as one of the seven dwarfs, Bashful, in the *Snow White* number. I wore a huge mask that covered my whole head and made it hard to see. My job became one of negotiating with the ice while tilting my head back as far as I could in order to see Dopey in front of me and not fall down and screw up the line. Adeline was a sugarplum fairy. Dad and Mom were pushing a sleigh.

My father was excited by our debut. When it was over and we were back home eating turkey sandwiches in the kitchen, he announced as he ladled out the homemade cranberry sauce, "Here's what we're going to do. You girls can put together a little act."

"What?" said Adeline.

"What do you mean?" I asked.

"You'll do a little pair skating together. Call it something. Get some music. It'll be fun! Do it at the Garden next year."

Adeline, the first to recover, said, "Daddy, I'm going to college."

"You can do that, too. Don't be a wet blanket."

"I'm not going anywhere," I said.

"See? You want to deprive your little sister of this opportunity? Here, have some more turkey. Peggy, pass your sister the cranberry sauce."

My father, being a doctor, probably knew about the sleep inducing attributes of the tryptophan in turkey. He was not only bribing her but drugging her as well.

In the end, Adeline was enlisted. We needed her. It couldn't happen without her.

Dad was passionate about figure skating.

"It's a helluva lot more graceful than ballet dancing," he said, driving home from the rink one night. "None of that stop-and-start stuff, trying to get your bearings after a jump or a spin. If you happen to fall down, you just keep going. The ice'll give you a slide. No hopping around on tortured feet in crippling toe shoes. You're wearing beautiful, white suede boots made to order by G. Stanzione, boot maker to the stars. You glide and flow on flashing silver blades. Fantasy blends into fantasy. It gives me chills. It's—I don't know—it's just indescribably glorious. It's fun. Connections can be made while you're having fun."

While I was trying to connect the dots of this final statement, a car cut across the lane in front of us and nearly caused a collision. Dad blew the horn, slowed down, muttered "Sonofabitch," and was quiet the rest of the way home.

We were swept up by his commitment, which was usually short-lived but this time seemed different. He wasn't going to lose interest and disappear this time, leaving us in the middle of a project for which we still needed him. Butterflies hatched in my stomach. We pitched in. We practiced our figure eights and threes and loops. We were deeply influenced, secondhand, by a disciple of Isadora Duncan. We called ourselves "The Wind and the Thistle." In a series of jumps and spins, a fox trot, a waltz, and a tango, Adeline as the Wind would chase me, the Thistle, around the rink as we channeled Isadora's principles of the free spirit. My father, at random, got a 78 rpm record off a shelf in his closet—"Walpurgisnacht (Witches' Night)" from Gounod's opera *Faust*—for our music.

He got us excused from school four afternoons a week to go into New York to practice. He drove over to the Kimberley school and flirted shamelessly with Miss Flannery, my homeroom teacher.

"Miss Flannery," he said, "may I have a moment of your valuable time?"

"Yes, Dr. Pope?" She wasn't sure. She was curious, though.

"Do you like pheasant?" he said. "I find it the most delicious fowl on the menu."

"Really?" said Miss Flannery. "I'm not all that familiar—"

"Oh, believe me. They are the best, and you know, I have a couple of them here that I felled from the skies of Pennsylvania for you. May I present them to you in honor of your work with my daughter, Peggy? She has grown so smart in your class this year. What a lovely cameo you're wearing."

"Why, thank you." Miss Flannery was totally flustered and would have granted my father any wish he might ask for after that.

My dad was the captain, my mother his first lieutenant. He assigned her to drive us into the city after school to rehearse. As we passed through the stench of the Jersey meadows and the pig farms of Secaucus, we rolled up the windows and ate a hot lunch in the Packard. The aromas of steamed vegetables and thermoses of tomato soup mixed with the leathery scent of our skating boots and filled the car. We changed our clothes as we ate so we'd be ready to step out and walk, with rubber guards on our skates, across the sidewalk, into the elevator, and directly on to the practice rink of Madison Square Garden. There we'd greet Miss Kasser in her mink coat and Robin Hood hat with the feather, and as the bell rang for the session to begin, we'd race to win a practice patch on the ice in front of the mirror before anybody else could get to it.

We created a scenario of the wind blowing a thistle across the ice for two minutes and thirteen seconds. That could be a very long time, depending on whether I fell down or not after the pull-through. There was a series of spins and jumps, the pull-through, and a speeding up toward the end so we could finish when the music did. I usually fell down following the pull-through because my father, concerned for my safety, had forbidden me to do it properly. The right way was to grab my sister's hands between her legs from behind, squat down, shoot one of my legs ahead, and lean back parallel to the ice while she pulled me through the bridge made by spreading her legs out wide.

Dad said to me, "You can't lie back flat because you could hit your head on the ice, knock yourself out, and end up an idiot for the rest of your life." Going through Adeline's legs in a hunched squat didn't work. I was too big and didn't fit under the bridge.

Meanwhile, my father had organized a number of out-of-town tryouts for us on the frozen putting greens of the golf clubs in New Jersey. We attracted audiences. Every time I fell down after the pull-through, I would slide and scramble to my feet amid gasps from the crowd. My sister was able to keep her balance throughout and, in a brilliant act of denial, improvise a distraction during the chaos. Beautiful and graceful, she'd twirl in an arabesque until I could pull myself together. Once, the fellow playing the record for us assumed we were finished after my fall and lifted the phonograph needle off our record. Without hesitation, Adeline, Sweet Adeline, sang the opening from *The Happy Farmer* as she did an extra swoop around the rink to cover for his gaffe as well as mine. But if nobody interfered, we would cut some of the dance steps and join up just as "Walpurgisnacht" scratched to a final crescendo.

After a while, Adeline started to lose interest—something about meeting boys going to college. She was five years older than I, and she had become distracted. Once in the car, she sat on "Walpurgisnacht," and it broke into shards. Unbeknownst to her, my dad and I had arranged to carry spares. It was a conspiracy, and she didn't have a chance. Nothing was going to stop the team.

In 1940, against the background of World War II, the war to end all wars, my father's perseverance was to pay off. We got a booking in New Haven. We were to perform during halftime at the Yale versus Brown game, the biggest college hockey game of the year.

Although I had stashed "Walpurgisnacht" in four separate places in the car, Adeline, worn out by her studies, decided to take a nap in the backseat. She stretched out, broke one record with her feet and one with her elbow, and then she smashed the other two when she dropped the carrying case on the way to the rink.

Yet there we were waiting on the ice between halves. The first half of the hockey game had been violent. Blood tinted the surface of the ice. It had become a soft pink that actually went well with our costumes. We waited for the man on the loudspeaker to explain about the Wind and the Thistle, about "Walpurgisnacht," about my father, about——.

"Adeline and Peggy Pope!" suddenly boomed out through the arena. There was no explanation. There was no music. The ice was not supposed to be bloody.

The startled fans on their way for beer and hot dogs turned, as if choreographed, to see a flash of silver chasing a bundle of lavender around a rosy rink in a sort of silent film.

I could sense their reaction. It enveloped me, made me feel like play dough and tipped me off that this was not an experience I wanted to have. But the Wind and the Thistle had a destiny. We didn't need an explanation, music, or Isadora Duncan. We went on. We were heroes like you see in the movies, soldiers going into battle facing certain death with heads held high, fierce, proud, loyal to the end.

When it was over, the audience seemed somewhat stunned. They sat like people on the subway waiting for the next stop. I looked for my father. He wasn't there. He'd gone to get the car. A sense of abandonment engulfed me. It was beginning to dawn on me that show business could be a tough racket.

A Couple of Stars Fall out

The Wind died down and the Thistle stopped spinning, and my brother Bruce died that summer. He had suffered for six years from colitis. Today they treat it with penicillin and can cure it quickly. In those days, before penicillin, they operated and operated and operated. The doctors didn't know what they were doing. And when Bruce came out of his sixth operation, he caught on to their charade. He was twenty-one when he said to my mom, who was sitting at his bedside in the hospital, "I don't want to live anymore."

He turned his head to the wall and died.

When my mom told me this, we were in Boston sitting side by side on my bed at the hotel in Boston. We were there to be close to Bruce in the hospital. She started to cry. I was twelve years old, and I had never seen her cry before. I had never seen any adult cry before. I was sitting very close to her, but she didn't hug me. I put my arm around her, which caused her to get up quickly and leave the room. I sat by myself for a while. Then I got my suitcase out and started packing.

Confined to the house for long recovery periods, Bruce had studied on his own with a tutor and taken the college boards in his bedroom. He had earned the highest marks and his pick of colleges. He had settled on Princeton or MIT. Now it didn't matter. He wasn't there to go anywhere.

The family ran aground after Bruce's death. My father's response was to drive himself even harder at work. I can see him coming across the front lawn in the evening, his brown overcoat, which he hadn't bothered to button, open and flapping, his beat-up medicine bag in his hand. He walked slowly, worn out from performing mastoid operations all day at the free clinic. Penicillin could have taken care of that problem, too. The following year, a heart attack would pick him off as well.

Nothing for it. Grin and bear it.

I turned thirteen that last year. Dad had begun delegating. He hired an instructor to teach me how to ride horseback. My mother usually took me to the lesson, but one hot day, my dad didn't go to work and took me to the riding academy himself.

"Stay in the ring," he said. "Don't go out on the trails. I'll be back."

My instructor, Mr. Fish, and I rode around the ring under the August sun until he said, "This is ridiculous. Nobody in their right mind rides around in circles under a sun like this." So off we went to the cool woods and trails of the reservation.

Mr. Fish was funny and made me laugh. I adored him. He was about forty with an open, clear face that stayed immobile whether he was giving instructions or encouragement or telling a joke. I had just said something funny myself, and we were both laughing when we got back to find Dad standing by the stable door. He looked distant, like a cop before he makes an arrest. Suddenly, my body went cold and then numb, and then I felt like needles were stabbing me everywhere.

"Go on. Get in the car. Go ahead now," he said from very far away.

He remained behind, chewing out Mr. Fish as I walked the long path to the parking area. I got in the front seat and waited. After what seemed like a day and a half, he came along and got in behind the wheel. He didn't start the car; he just sat looking straight ahead. I could see he was trying to control his rage, find his balance. His face was so red that he looked like he was going to explode. Gripping the wheel and clenching his teeth, he might as well have been a character in the funny papers with a balloon above his head saying, "#'X!?#!*!"

"What did you think you were doing?" he finally said.

"I don't know," I said. "Mr. Fish said it would be all right, that it was perfectly safe." I started to sob. "That I was ready to do it."

"I'll tell you when you're ready. Not some goddamned instructor. You're not old enough to go cavorting around in the woods with that bastard. Who the hell does he think he is? You're a child, for God's sake! You're a little girl, and he's a grown man! He has no business taking you into the woods!"

It was hot in the car. The sun had moved, taking the shade of the tree with it.

Sweat covered his face, but he paid no attention to it. His voice rose, but I couldn't make out what he was saying. The August heat made the stables shimmy in the distance. The sun glared on the car hood, hit the white fence around the riding ring, and blinded my eyes. He ranted. The air stopped moving. The trees stood at attention. A free-range turkey strutted by, unaware of its future. He roared on and reached a decibel level that made me cover my ears. I stopped crying. He was going to use up all the oxygen in the car with his yelling, but I didn't move or open my window. I could see the headlines: "Hottest Day of the Year; Father and Daughter Cooked in Car." I could no longer hear him. His mouth was moving, but there was no sound. Still looking straight ahead, hands white-knuckled on the wheel, he saw the turkey crossing in front of him. He tried to swerve to avoid hitting it before he realized the car wasn't moving. It was then that I fell asleep.

*   *   *

My father died that November, one morning shortly before his birthday. He had been out in the yard rigging up a run for the new dog, a springer spaniel named Buck who was going to go hunting with us the next week. Dad went into the house and upstairs, where he told my mom that he didn't feel well and went into their bedroom to lie down. She called his friend Dr. Synott, who came right over, but again, in those days there was nothing he could do to save Dad.

My mother met me at the front door when I came home from school. I followed her into the dining room, where she stopped in front of the sideboard. We stood there in front of the picture of Jim and Bruce as babies in white gowns playing beside a fish pond. I was fingering a crocheted lace runner as she said, "He's gone." I didn't respond. I just stood there. Suddenly, she threw her arms around me, then just as suddenly pulled away and ran upstairs. After a while, I went into the kitchen, where I ran into Nellie, the cook, who wanted to comfort me and hug me. I broke away from her and ran up the back stairs to my room.

Later that day, I stood in my dad's study, next to my parents' bedroom, where he was lying. My report card lay on his desk, unsigned. I had gotten all the A's he had ordered. It came to me that if I went in where he was and kissed him on the lips, he would come back to life. I didn't do it. Years later, I told a group of people about the shame I felt about this fantasy, and one of the women said, "Oh, yes. That happened to me, too."

*   *   *

Twelve years after his death, my father came to see me in my first appearance on Broadway. The play was *Moonbirds* by Marcel Aymé. It starred Wally Cox and Sir Michael Hordern. I was the ingénue in this French farce, so naturally my second entrance was in a merry widow corset. While I was onstage stealing the scene, I saw a man sitting in the first row studying me. He frightened me. I wished he would go away. *Who was he? A critic? No, a critic would be wearing a jacket and taking notes.* This man looked as if he had just been working in the garden. He possessed a power that threatened to paralyze me.

A chill charged through me, and I saw that it was my father sitting there—not a ghost, but very real. For a moment, I thought I was going to faint. All my life I had been performing for him. All my life he had been there egging me on and then leaving just when I needed him to stay.

So now what's he up to? Is he always going to show up and sit there? Let me know I'm just a little kid still? Suddenly, my fantasy saved me. Strength rose in me and led me to drive him out of his seat, will him up the aisle and through the exit door, and kick him out of the theater. I went on with the scene.

He still comes back to haunt me, telling me to stay small, hide, apologize, get his permission, acknowledge his authority. But I'm okay; I watch out. I point to the exit, and to my amazement, he goes.

Mom On-stage

One night my mother put on her Montclair hat, the high-crowned tweed, over her curling rods before she came to pick me up at Miss Sawyer's Dancing School. The curlers were large and formed what looked like a hat itself. The tweed looked like a second hat on top of them. When I asked her the next day how she could appear like that in public, she said, "It was dark and raining, and I didn't think anyone would notice."

That was the night Bumble had asked me to join him for the last dance. Bumble was tall and skinny and had curly, dark brown hair. He had a gawky walk, and I could hear Felix the Cat cartoon music as he beelined across the dance floor to me. Then he did his Jimmy Cagney impression: "Wanna dance, kid? Shake a leg, maybe?" I said, "Why, yes, I'd love to, ya big lug." We slow-danced off.

When he asked if he could drive me home, I told him my mother was coming for me, so he offered to escort me through the rain to my carriage. We were Scarlett and Rhett leaving the ball. He held his coat over my head as we walked along the driveway, protecting me from the storm, looking for my mom.

As my mother pulled up, backlit by the lights of the car behind her, she became a two-headed silhouette, one head growing out of the other. Bumble was not prepared for her. He took Kay Watt home the next week and didn't ask me to dance again.

"He is the first regret of my life," I said.

"He doesn't have enough inner resources," Mom said.

*　　　　*　　　　*

I was fifteen when my mother and I, in an effort to recapture some of the fun we'd had at the shore back when we were a family, took a trip to the beach. This was before swimming caps were covered with rubber flowers. My mother put on a plain white one as we faced the breakers on an empty Long Island beach. We dove into one that was higher than we had expected and were immediately knocked down and dragged away from the shore. We were rolled and mixed with the sand, the seaweed, and the horseshoe crabs. The air was pounded out of us, and water stuffed our noses and throats. The ground switched from above to below us and back again, making it impossible to get our footing. I saw my mother, her white cap gone, being pulled out to sea; she was caught in the undertow of the ebbing wave. I tried to grab her but missed. She disappeared into another wave and then reappeared, and I grabbed again. That time, I got hold of her. In a valley between waves, salt scraping my eyes, I got my head into the air, coughed, and spit until my lungs started working again. Then, gripping her wrist, I dragged her onto the beach, where we lay in the hard sunlight next to a giant timber from a ship that had been washed up just ahead of us.

I lay there thinking of my mother's hats and how when she went ice skating, she wore a red band around her head to keep her hair in place. I loved my mother in red. She wasn't much of a skater, but she was game and would skate around the edge of the rink while my father waltzed, fox-trotted, and tangoed in the center with the other women in the club. Once in a while, he'd go over and waltz with her, but it was a shaky affair. It was too late in her life for her to become an athlete. She had been so beautiful that she'd never been called upon to be anything else.

I loved my mother in her black evening dress with the red poppies on it. Her innate wisdom couldn't be matched, and her naïveté had always protected her. She had a good mind and loved to laugh, but when Bruce died and my father followed the next year, she became lost, left alone with only me in a three-story house that used to be full of servants, children, company, various dogs, and my father. Now it was hard to keep going.

I loved my mother in her cornflower-blue evening dress that she wore with her pearl dangle earrings. I can smell the French perfume she would dab behind her ears. Essence of Héliotrope Blanc, contained in a miniature crystal whiskey decanter, stood faithfully on her dresser at the ready.

Oh, please Mom, I would think, *make some friends and get a life and let me go.* She couldn't do that. She clung to me, and I squirmed away.

I loved my mom in her New York hat with the breathtaking wide brim and the "I dare you" red wooden cherries on it.

Some time after the near-drowning incident, I stood in the driveway with her under the cherry tree as its blossoms blew away on the spring breeze. She wasn't wearing any hat at all. She said, "When I die, I'd like to go like that, just like a leaf floating on the wind."

Then she said, "My wedding dress is on the shelf in my closet. I'd like to be buried in it."

She believed she was going to see them again, Bruce and Dad.

Aunt Bea Spills the Beans

My apartment on the Upper West Side at tea time.

My Aunt Bea started it.

"You know your father had a log cabin on top of the old Hotel Nassau?"

"In Manhattan?"

"Thirty-fourth and Lexington."

"I never knew that."

"Nobody in your family knew it."

"Mom would have known."

"Your mother didn't know anything."

"How did you know?"

"He invited your uncle Gardiner to dinner there when I was in the hospital."

"I don't believe this!"

"It's true. Gardiner told me about it. Could I have another cookie? They are so——"

"What! What did he tell you?"

"Oh, I probably shouldn't have——"

"Tell me!"

"Well, it was a snowy night, and Ed said, 'Come on, Gardiner. I'll blow you to dinner.' They went to the Hotel Nassau, up in the elevator and out on the roof, and there, sitting in the middle of the snow, was a log cabin with smoke coming out of its chimney. They could have been way off in the woods somewhere if it hadn't been for the water tower. They went inside, and there were candles on the table, a white linen tablecloth, silver dinnerware, and a colored maid to serve them. How about some more coffee?"

I went into the kitchen. I had no idea my father had spread himself so thin. Here's what I knew about my father. He was a doctor. He thought he was going to live forever, so when he died we had to pay a double inheritance tax: one in New Jersey, where we lived, and one in New York, where he practiced because he wanted to be able to vote wherever he was and influence everyone he could.

I came back to the living room with coffee and cookies for my aunt.

"Is that where they had dinner?"

"Lovely dinner. Cocktails, roast chicken, salad, apple pie."

"Goodness."

"Coffee. Brandy."

"Did Uncle Gardiner tell you this?"

"Gardiner told me everything."

"Did you tell Mom?"

"Of course not. What do you think I am?"

"Why are you telling me?"

"Well, it's all ancient history now, don'cha know?"

"I suppose. You think he had trysts there?" I said.

"You tell me."

Aunt Bea looked at me sideways.

"I guess with the candles and all . . . I know he used to get a red rose delivered to him every Christmas. One year the rose came and it was withered, and then no more after that. He and Mom had a huge fight about it, doors slamming and everything."

"You don't say."

In the silence Aunt Bea reached for a cookie and popped it into her mouth. *Crunch*

. . . *crunch.* She brushed her fingertips together to get rid of the crumbs. Her manicured hand was covered with age spots.

This revelation of Dad's secret other life made me shake inside. *Why didn't we know this about my dad?* I needed to breathe. I needed my Aunt Bea to go home.

"Did Uncle Gardiner tell you about the bathtub gin and the FBI?" I said.

She stopped mid-bite and squinted at me. Her silver-rimmed glasses reflected the setting sun from the window behind me.

I said, "Well, what we knew was that Dad had access to medical alcohol. Mr. McCarthy, the manager of the Hotel Nassau, had access to empty rooms with bathtubs. They'd meet on Saturday afternoons and make gin."

"Never heard that."

"Oh, yes," I said, "and one afternoon when they were busy in the bathroom, the desk clerk rang to say FBI men were on their way up with a search warrant. So Dad and Mr. McCarthy turned into Laurel and Hardy, stumbling over each other to hide the apparatus and pull the plug out of the tub. The last of the gin went *glug glug glug* down the drain just as there was a knock on the door. Mr. Mac opened it. Two men flashed their badges and asked him if he was the manager. He said he was, and how could he help them?

"One of them said in a low voice, 'We have a warrant for the arrest of some counterfeiters we believe are in the room next door.' Mr. McCarthy whispered back, 'Be my guest. Here's my passkey.' The counterfeiters were taken away, and Dad and Mr. Mac were still at large, minus a bathtub full of gin."

Aunt Bea sat stunned. How had she missed this? What else had Uncle Gardiner kept from her? The room had grown dark.

"That was excellent gin," she said. I could see she remembered it. She sighed and said, "Where's my hat?"

*   *   *

Later, after she'd gone, as I was doing the dishes, images of my dad bounced around in my head. When I was five, I thought he was a train conductor on the New York Ioneer. Great trains had names like that in those days: the Northwest Commander, the Southern Pacific, the New York Ioneer.

"He's not a conductor. He's a *doctor*," said my mother.

"On a train?" I said.

"No, he takes the train to the New York Eye and Ear Hospital."

"Why does an eye and ear need a whole hospital?" I said.

My mother, who was driving the car at the time, said, "Sweetie, I can't talk to you just now. I have to make a turn." It was a lot for me to keep up with.

Dad was usually late for his train because he'd have been in the backyard looking at his roses. At the last minute there was a mad scramble of running up and down stairs, dogs barking, my mother calling, "Ed, I'll go warm up the car!" and Dad answering, "Where's my bag, Margaret?" "Just where you left it!" she'd call back, and the screen door would slam and she'd start *crunch crunch*ing on the gravel to the garage while he looked for his bag in the closet upstairs and I'd look in the hall closet where he usually left it. Finally one of us would find it, and the three of us would end up in the Packard chasing the De Camp Bus because he'd missed the train. After he was safely on the bus, my mother and I would turn to each other and sing, "De Camptown Race Train five miles long, oh de doo-dah day."

My father raised money for the new hospital where he served as executive surgeon. He worked long hours and donated his services to the clinic once a week. The porous mastoid bone behind the ear can get infected in cold and flu season or from swimming in public pools. In those days, it had to be drained in a delicate procedure, and Dad could perform up to fifteen mastoid operations a day. Today that procedure has been replaced by a dose of antibiotics. Out in the world, my dad was beloved by all for his generosity, good looks, and charm.

Sometimes he'd call from New York to tell my mother that he wouldn't be home for dinner—not often, but enough that I remember it.

Coming home, he was on his own. He'd take the crosstown bus and a downtown subway and then stop at the Washington Market. He'd pick up some Roquefort cheese, consider the moose head on the wall behind the butcher, and then hop on the ferry to Hoboken, where he'd call my mother to tell her which train he'd be taking. Then he'd buy a paper and board the DL&W. commuter train (dubbed by us the Delay, Linger, and Wait). There he'd take a seat and proceed to get furious with the "commie pinkos," Max Lerner, and the *World-Telegram*. I can hear him muttering "Dog-eat-dog" and "Sonofabitch, country's a shipwreck." No wonder he sometimes went to his log cabin instead.

Learning Curves: The Elegance of Lisping

I had a year of Latin at the Kimberley Day School for Girls. *Educare* is a Latin verb that means "to lead out." What a wonderful way to look at learning: A good teacher can open a door and lead you out of your "not knowing."

In the beginning was my kindergarten teacher, Miss Sargent—tall and beautiful, a ready smile, the sound of her voice like a song, a lullaby of reassurance that she would always be there to take care of us. Even the goldfish on the bookcase stopped swimming to look at her when she was teaching. I have no memory of what she taught us. It could have been calculus and we would have learned it. We loved her so and would have done anything for her. She loved us, too, we thought, but she pulled the rug out from under us after spring vacation when she showed us her engagement ring and said she was leaving us at the end of the month. It seemed she was just passing through on her way to a better life that wouldn't include us. She couldn't wait to be rid of us. Betrayal and abandonment! We could get that at home.

One day she took off her engagement ring to wash her hands and left it on the sink in the school bathroom. It sparkled; it beckoned; it practically danced. When Cynthia Youngman picked it up to look at it, she accidentally dropped it, and as I watched, it rolled down the drain. Later, when Miss Sargent asked the class if any of us had seen it, whether we had been at the scene of the crime, we all said no. *Why should we help her find it?* We wanted revenge. She didn't want to play with us anymore? Well, she wasn't *our* friend. In the slang of the day, we "fixed her wagon." She was going to have a lot of explaining to do that night. Miss Sargent had not led us out. She had led us on, a good teacher gone bad.

In fifth grade, an ancient Alice Woodward had a passion for teaching so strong that she drooled when she taught *Macbeth*. Inspired by her enthusiasm and the play's blood and gore, I wrote a story in her class about shooting and killing a pheasant while hunting with my father. I told how I had shot the bird in its left wing and it had jerked in the air and swerved and coasted down into a grove of trees, where we never found it. My father said, "Better to kill him immediately. You don't want to make him suffer." I was haunted by what I had done. I couldn't stop thinking about it. It was a current of shame running through my days, and my story sprang from that.

Miss Woodward loved the tale and urged me to send it to *Junior Scholastic* magazine. It was published. I was startled by this event. She told me to write more, but I never could. I didn't know how I'd done it, so I didn't know how to do it again. And Miss Woodward didn't have a clue. Her method of passing on knowledge was no help with the creative process. She didn't know about art. She only knew what she liked. The craft of tapping into my intuition and writing and the task of leading me out of my writer's block were beyond her.

So I kept my achievement a secret. I had revealed personal stuff—feelings, vulnerability—stuff I couldn't deal with. *Was I too different? Did it show? Was there something wrong with me?* I wanted to be like everybody else with a normal family. My mother, coming across my published story years later, said to me, "I never knew you felt that way." But hadn't she told me, "If you don't give voice to something, it will go away"? Of course, she'd been talking about gossip—or had she? Between Miss Woodward and my mother and the memory of my father's world philosophy, I developed a major neurosis called Sit on Everything. Rage walked in to fill in the blanks.

At the Kimberley Day School for Girls, we wore the school uniform: green skirts, matching sweaters, yellow blouses with Peter Pan collars, and saddle shoes or loafers. We looked more or less alike. (Weezy Rudd recently sent me a class picture to try to persuade me to come to a reunion, and I couldn't find myself in it.)

One spring feverish day, I sat amid this sea of green and yellow, a part of it and yet not, at a wooden desk with a raise-up lid. Miss Flannery, our seventh grade teacher, a big woman with sagging skin and jowls that flapped when she shook her head, was talking about I-don't-know-what in a voice that sounded like Jell-O. She had created a boredom so deep in the room that my attention drifted to the window and the chain-link fence surrounding the school outside.

Nancy Hollenbeck, who may have grown up to be a football coach, sat behind me. We were close enough that I was always able to get any information I needed from her quickly and unobtrusively. "Nancy, what are those birds doing on that fence?" I asked her. "One of them is on top of the other. What's going on?" I was alarmed for them, especially the one on the bottom.

I can't remember exactly what she said or how she said it, but I was horrified to hear it. I felt trapped. I couldn't take it in. I couldn't move. I didn't know what to do about it. I didn't know if I should keep watching. I didn't know if Nancy Hollenbeck was telling me the truth.

"What?" I said.

"They're fucking," she said out loud while Miss Flannery wrote on the blackboard.

"What, dear?" said Miss Flannery, turning but unable to identify anyone in the green-and-yellow blur. The room was silent. Alas, learning in Miss Flannery's class always happened by accident.

It was spring, and I suddenly didn't want to learn anything more, ever. At recess, the teachers were having their weekly faculty meeting in the Latin teachers' room, and as I walked by the closed door, I saw a brass key sticking out of it. I turned and walked by it again. On the third pass, I stopped and locked all those terrible teachers in the room where the blackboards were covered with Latin. We had an extended recess that day, and I used the time to pull myself together. If the gym teacher hadn't climbed out the window, if the room had been on the second floor, they'd still be there, rotting away, their teeth falling out. They knew better than to ask who did it. They knew they had lost the day.

Then it occurred to me that if I lowered my sights just a hair, I could be Rosalind Russell, who had played Amelia Earhart in the movie. *I could be an actress!* When I was grown up, when I was twenty-one, I could go to New York just across the river and be somebody else there, not the dreary Gloomy Gus I felt I had become. An actress! That's the ticket. Actresses can be all sorts of people. I could be a hero on a stage! I could hide there.

When I was sixteen, I got a part in the local drama club's production of *The Night of January 16th.* It was a small part, as a witness at a murder trial. It didn't matter; I was in a show. However, after a few rehearsals, I discovered that the short role of a witness on a stand wasn't very interesting. Then, out of nowhere, it came to me: *What if it was really hard for her to sit in this chair and answer questions in front of a group of strangers? Why would that be? Is there something special, something special about . . . How about . . . What if she . . . What if she had a lisp?*

When I lisped during the next rehearsal, it was so funny that everybody in the room cracked up. The rehearsal came to a halt, and the director shouted, "This is a murder trial, not a comedy! Cut that out."

Yet it was so much fun while it lasted that I thought later, *I've never had such a good time. That's what I want to do for the rest of my life.* It felt like flying. I felt like someone else. I felt like this lispy witness and me at the same time. It was almost like being possessed. I felt no responsibility for what I said or did. It was all being taken care of for me. And that's what can happen; one simple adjustment in the body or the attitude can do all that. What a pleasure!

In my final year of high school, I had the opportunity to meet and learn about boys. At Miss Sawyer's Dancing School, the students from the Montclair Academy for Boys were our partners one Saturday night a month for ten months. It was too late in life for me to get the hang of it. I tried. I read *The Ethel Cotton Course in Conversation* that my sister, Adeline, had sent away for and used a few years earlier. But it didn't help. Ethel Cotton was living in an Edith Wharton novel. She suggested I read the newspaper and introduce topics from there, but I needed smart banter and lively comebacks. I didn't realize this until I heard myself saying once during a slow fox-trot, "So what do you think of the war?" My partner just stared at me. Another dance step in the wrong direction.

My mother had taken me shopping for an evening gown at Best and Company in East Orange, and between us we had picked something in a taffeta plaid because it seemed "cheerful." Everyone else was in soft, flowing pastels. I felt like Ida Lupino in reverse, when she went to that picnic on the farm in an evening dress.

Having to hang around near the wall and wait to be asked to dance was agony mixed with shame. Years later I was ranting about this over supper at a summer share in a beach house when a man yelled at me, "How do you think it felt for us? All night long I had to schlep across that floor, go up to a girl and ask, 'May I have this dance?' She'd bray out a 'No!' you could hear all over the room, and I hadda murble the whole way back where I came from and start over again."

I was flabbergasted to think that this had never occurred to me, that life might be excruciating for everybody.

The Loony Bin

Back in the fifties, one rain-filled February afternoon, Lynn Anderson surprised me. She said to Annie, Dee, Biz Greenman, and me, all actresses in the Smith College theater department, that she'd like to go over to the VA hospital and meet the men in the psychiatric ward.

"It occurred to me," she said as she folded up the ground cloth that kept the costumes clean while she pinned them on us, "that it might be a good thing to do a play with them." She let that sink in, and then she said. "Not *for* them. *With* them."

We never questioned why she wanted to put on a play in a loony bin. We got on the bus and went with her because our thirst for acting was not being slaked at Smith. Playing Romeo to Lorna Landis's Juliet in Miss Sickles's speech class was not paying off for me.

We knew the hospital from driving by it on our way from Smith to parties at Amherst on the weekends. It was an isolated building, hugging the ground behind a chain-link fence, a war scar on a Massachusetts back road. It was full of damaged men that Uncle Sam no longer wanted.

Each time we passed it, someone would call out, "Loony bin!" like a conductor on an express bus passing a local stop that nobody needed—and I would wonder what went on in there. Was it a Charles Addams cartoon place where men like Uncle Fester swept the halls? Did patients getting shock treatments scream behind locked doors? Was the man I was destined to have married among them, in there weaving baskets?

And then we'd be at the dreaded frat house, where the awkward lechery of the Eligible Young Men from Good Families would be released upon us. Young chaps chug-a-lugging beer, honing their drinking abilities, were waiting for us, their ids at attention, waiting to pounce.

Lynn rescued us from this hospitality. A grad student on a grant, getting a degree in costume design, she had chosen not to patronize the "Amherst zoo." She preferred to spend her weekends in the basement workroom of the theater building in service to her art, her lanky frame hunched over a sewing machine. She wore wire-rimmed glasses and rarely combed her mouse-brown hair. She never wore makeup. Fabric and watercolor sketches covered the table and walls. A headless manikin oversaw the creation of costumes for the shows.

On occasion, a fellow grad student would drop by, desperate for a cigarette. Lynn didn't smoke, although Annie thought it would be a good idea if she did, especially during costume fittings. Her passion for her work was accompanied by a temper and it didn't help when we would argue with her as we picked through her offerings. We never considered the period of the play. We were concerned with how we looked in the mirror. A higher heel, a shorter skirt, a lower neckline was what we wanted, as well as an upswept hairdo—not some dumb hat.

The veterans were waiting for us in the main hall. Dull light from the barred windows near the ceiling shafted through the dust of the tall room. Swaths of plaster waved to us as they peeled from the walls, and giant spider webs draped the corners. Two broken-down wheelchairs were propped against each other at the entrance. A card table and a chair sat by the door that led into the entrails of the building.

The men looked like a ragtag bunch of overtall children, eager to play with us. Some had been there for years. They made me think of my Uncle Paul, who had become shell-shocked in World War I. He had spells of violence that were unpredictable and had to be "sent away" until he got over them, sent to a place like this, maybe. He used to visit us sometimes in Montclair. He looked like Teddy Roosevelt—huge, in a brown tweed suit. He would sit on the Queen Anne ladies chair in the living room, his hands holding each other as if to keep himself from flying apart. He never said much. If you mentioned to him that he had been in the war, he would say, "Was I?"

Then he'd rub his temples with the heels of his hands as if to bring back the memory. When he couldn't do it, he'd drift off again into a cloud of lost interest.

I had told Lynn about Uncle Paul. "Because of him," I said, "although I was only eight or nine at the time, I feel especially qualified for this project. Doing a play with mental patients would be right up my alley."

She looked at me for a long moment, at the end of which she said, "Oh, good."

A woman wearing a nurse's cap, a print dress, and low-heeled shoes had assembled our cast for us.

"Here we are, boys," she said. "This is your contingent, Miss Anderson."

She read from her clipboard as if it were a laundry list. "Irving. Tom. George—" She looked up, caught them all gazing at us, and said, "Step forward when I call your name, boys. Irving. Tom. George. Sam—" Sam didn't budge. Sam, in overalls and a dark, long-sleeved work shirt, stood by himself staring at something that wasn't there. He looked like a scarecrow in a field of scattered cornstalks.

"Never mind, Sam," said the nurse, going right on. "Dave, Alec, and Fish. There may be a few more next time if you need them. They may come and go. We'll see."

Irving took a second step forward. He looked and sounded like Jimmie Durante, with the same big nose and gravelly voice.

"Pleased to meet you," he said. "I, personally, am staying."

"Oh, good," said Lynn. "I'm going to put you in charge, my second in command. Is that okay with you, Irving?"

"Definitely. At your service. What's *your* name?" he said. He had dressed for the event: khakis, a blue sweater, and a lapel pin—a tiny eagle that the Army gave soldiers when they were discharged. The soldiers called it a ruptured duck, and Irving had polished his till it gleamed.

"Oh, excuse me. I'm so sorry." Lynn immediately introduced herself and us, and the men brightened. Irving caught me watching Sam, who hadn't spoken.

"Don't worry about Sam," said Irving. "He's okay. He's the best. He'll grow on you."

"Do you have an auditorium?" Lynn asked the nurse.

"Yes, we do," said the nurse. "This used to be a school, you know, until someone decided it was ready to fall down and unsafe for children. Follow me."

We walked through a maze of hallways to a dusty and unused auditorium.

There was no curtain or wings or backstage, just a large, raised rectangle stuck in one end of the room. On it, a podium, an upright piano, and a bunch of chairs stood at odd angles to one another. A crushed volleyball lay in the far corner. A ragged center aisle was suggested by straight-backed chairs, which we guessed we would probably have to dust off ourselves.

"This is wonderful," said Lynn. "Let's get to work."

"I'll be leaving you, then," said the nurse,

Without thinking, Lynn said, "Oh, please do!"

When the nurse pursed her lips and raised her eyebrows, Lynn kept going.

"I didn't mean that the way it sounded. I am so sorry. I mean, ah, um . . . Thank you so much. You've been so, um——"

"I'll be back later to see how it's working out," the nurse said before she walked away, sniffing.

Lynn took a deep breath to even herself out and said, "Oh-kaay. I've got a bunch of scripts here, but let me just tell you what this story's about."

"Yeah, what's it about?" said Irving.

"Good idea. All aboard," said Dave, a wiry elf of a fellow. He had a scruffy white beard and was a wearing a trainman's hat.

"It's about Johnny Appleseed, a folk hero."

"Johnny Appleseed?" Tom said. He had a round, ruddy face framed by white hair, although he could have been my age.

"Yes," said Lynn. "He walked across the country with a bag of apple seeds on his back."

"Excellent," said Fish, thin and gangly, a head taller than the rest.

They began to gather around, caught up in her enthusiasm.

"Yes! A man with a dream," said Lynn, and she told them how after the American Revolution, he had walked all the way from New York to Illinois, planting apple seeds. All by himself. He was a legend. He cleared land in the wilderness. He made friends with the Indians. He made friends with wild animals. He had to. One winter it was so cold that he shared a cave with a bear. In the spring, he sold the seedlings to the settlers for whatever they wanted to give him. Great orchards that are still alive today sprang up.

Lynn raised her arms and made tiny circles in the air with her hands as she spoke.

"Orchards. What a good idea." said Fish. "What's your name again?"

"Come on over here, Sam. Join us," said Irving, drawing him into the group. Sam held on to Irving's coat.

"Meet my friends, three Indians and a wild bear," said Dave, pulling on his beard. He and Fish started to do Indian war whoops, and young Tom, playing a bear, growled at them.

"I give you Johnny Appleseed. A legend in his own mind," said Tom.

I could feel the air pulsing. Lynn kept us going.

"Okay, okay, calm down, everybody," she said. "I see you all can act. Now listen to these songs and see which ones you like."

Annie slammed right into "Greensleeves" on a piano so out of tune it made us howl. She played on, and Tom, his white hair flying, sang out in a strong, musical voice. George, a fat, high baritone, and Fish, a rich bass in a long body, joined him. Irving could talk-sing anything. We were all singing. We had to. We had to drown out the piano. That is, all except for Sam, who stayed by Irving, quietly listening, staring.

Our rehearsal time came to an end. Lynn gave out the scripts and said, "Don't lose them. I had to type them all myself. Are there any questions?"

"Yeah," said George. "What do you eat at Smith?"

Of all the veterans we had met, he reminded me the most of Uncle Paul, if a bit heavier and able to ask a question—especially if it was about food. He was particularly interested in desserts. I told him our favorite dessert was called Football.

"What's that?" he said.

"It's a sweet, brown cake," I said, "with the texture of a muffin and the size of a football, with chocolate seams. But it's only as good as the amount of whipped cream you put on it. And that's usually gone before it's halfway round the table."

"Oh, could you bring me some?" he said. "With a lot of whipped cream?"

"You bet." I had a feeling that we were on the verge of becoming best friends.

As we left, thinking we were out of earshot, I said to Lynn, "What about Sam?"

But Irving was right behind us.

"Sam can sing," he said, making me jump. "He just takes some warming up. He should have a solo."

"A *solo*?" said Lynn.

"I've heard him many times. Alec plays the guitar. Sam sings when Alec plays."

"I see," said Lynn

"What's wrong with him?" I asked.

"*Peggy!*" Lynn glared at me.

"He's what they call catatonic," said Irving. "He's been like that for a few years. He'll pull out of it one of these days. He had a bad experience in the war."

He looked back down the hall and saw the nurse waving at him.

"To be continued," he said. "Adios."

On our way back in the bus, Dee, who was minoring in French, said in her solid New York accent, "Well, that was *très intéressant.*"

"We better get that piano tuned before they learn the wrong melodies," said Annie.

"And what about Sam?" I said. "He's kind of scary, isn't he? He looks like an ax murderer."

"Don't worry, Peggy," said Lynn. "It's going to work out." Then she sighed, put her head against the window, and fell asleep. We kept quiet after that. I don't know about the others, but in the silence, it came to me that for a loner, Lynn had been pretty impressive that day and deserved more respect from us.

*　　　　*　　　　*

I saw the show as a vehicle for me. I played Pocahontas, dancing and singing in a performance that would take your breath away. I saw it as the launching of a major career. I would stop the show in my orange-and-white beaded outfit, the top elegantly reaching to mid-thigh, an eagle with out-spread wings across the back of the tunic, the skirt ending at a sexy curve in my calf. Add a beaded headband with obligatory feather: Fabulous! Nobody in this loony bin would guess it came from the twenties, mis-catalogued by the Smith wardrobe department. This was turning into a very freeing experience for me.

A producer on a weekend getaway would be in the audience. He would discover me, and I would excuse myself early from college to go to New York to be in his show. "Pack up all my care and woe. Hang on, Broadway, here I go. Blackbird, bye-bye!"

The veterans took to the story of Johnny Appleseed and fell in love with us. They couldn't do enough for us. At one early rehearsal, Fish offered us a pumped-up volleyball and a neatly folded net.

"Can we use these in the show?"

"Maybe," said Lynn, her face clouding over. Then she grinned. "Sure, why not?"

"There was a guy used to come here," said Fish. "He was writing a thesis. He brought us this volleyball and net and organized a game every week."

"What happened to him?" said Lynn.

"He got his degree and left for a while."

"That's too bad," said Lynn.

"Then the net disappeared. Yeah, I've been looking for this net for some time."

"Where was it?"

"In a room off the kitchen," said Irving. "The cook was using it to store pots and pans. I had a helluva time getting it away from him. Finally I said, 'I'd hate for that guy to come back and find out what happened to his net.' So the cook gave it to me."

"Well, we'll definitely find a place for some volleyball in *Johnny Appleseed*," said Lynn. "Hey, we could use it as a warm-up for the show."

Fish, a Cheshire cat smile topping his great height, said, "We had a pretty good team," and he dribbled the ball around the auditorium, showing off. "Hey, guys, gimme a hand." A suddenly reconstituted team pushed back some chairs and joined him. They were bouncing and passing that ball all over the place. Their energy heated up the hall, which had been cold a few minutes before. Now the room was shaking and everybody was laughing.

At the next rehearsal, Irving showed up as the Spirit of '76 in a costume he'd designed. He'd draped himself in rags and bound his head up in a white bandage. He carried a flag and two wooden sticks and played a drumroll on the back of a chair.

"A man and his dream, right?" he said.

Sam kept hanging around by himself, not about to knock us out with his singing. Irving, still in his Spirit of '76 regalia drew Lynn aside on a break and said, "Here's the thing, Lynn. Don't worry about Sam. He's gonna sing."

"*When?*" asked Lynn.

"Calm down. Calm down," said Irving. "Here's what we need to do."

Lynn took a deep breath and said, "Okay. What?"

"He has a beautiful tenor voice," said Irving. "We should . . . we should have him stand onstage during rehearsals, and we'll all act around him. By the time we open, he'll be singing a song. I guarantee it."

"How can you be so sure of that?"

"I know him. I was in his company, his unit." Irving heaved a great sigh. "Okay. Eight years ago. WWII. Island-hopping in the Pacific—Tarawa Island, to be exact. One night he got separated from the unit, one night in the jungle, and he happened on some enemy soldiers, surprising them. He took them prisoner, all thirty-three of them, single-handedly. A regular Audie Murphy. He was going to bring them back to the base, but he was overcome by fatigue. He knew if he fell asleep, see, they would kill him."

Irving paused and checked for eavesdroppers. He and Lynn and I were the only ones in the hallway. He went on, keeping his voice low.

"So he shot them all. When dawn came, he found his way back to the base. He told his sergeant what had happened, lay down on a cot in the infirmary, and fell asleep for three days. He hasn't spoken since. But I swear to you, stack of Bibles, sometimes I hear him singing a little tune, and it's beautiful. He has a beautiful voice."

It was quiet for a moment. Then Lynn looked Irving in the eye. There was no way for us to know if this tale was true, exaggerated, imagined, or dreamed.

"And now he's going to sing—in the show?" she said.

"Of course. He's gonna sing in the show. Why wouldn't he sing in the show?

Just put him up there in the center of the stage and tell him to sing "Danny Boy!" Come on. We gotta rehearse."

We tried it. When it came time for Sam's song, Alec brought out a guitar and played it for him. Sam stood there, arms hanging limp, eyes set too deep to reflect the light, hair stringy, voice silent.

A few more rehearsals went by like this.

On the bus one evening Biz, our stage manager, said, "What if it doesn't happen? What do I do for a cue?"

"*Mais oui. Quel dommage s'il ne chant pas!*" said Dee.

"I could play the song, and it might look like he was thinking it," said Annie. "He pretty much looks like that anyway."

"*S'il n'a pas parlé depuis huit ans, pourquoi chanterait-il maintenant?*" asked Dee. And then, "Hey, I just made a rhyme in French!"

"Maybe he's forgotten the words," said Biz.

"He could hum them," I said.

There was an element of hysteria in our giggles.

"Oh, shut up!" said Lynn. "You're driving me nuts!"

Lynn sat in the rear of the bus, her jaw clenched, her temples pulsing. She said, "I can't begin to tell you how much I really hate each and every one of you right now. And maybe forever!"

We got quiet.

In rehearsal the following day, Sam sang something—a word—a syllable—. It was a single sound. It had a primitive, groaning-door quality to it. It scraped over us. We stood very still, waiting, wanting. But there was nothing more, just the guitar.

When Alec came to the end of the song, Irving went over to Sam. "That's it, Sam," he said, patting him on the shoulder. "Keep going. 'Danny Boy.' What a great song."

Little by little, singing a word here and a word there—a few more each time we met—Sam was rehearsing a miracle. The scarecrow was leaving, and a man was emerging. The day he put the first three words together, "Oh, Danny Boy," he was truly the Irish farmer during the Great Famine saying good-bye to his son. He was a natural. Annie, on the piano, joined Alec very quietly to swell the music. A tiny crack of a smile threatened to sneak across Sam's face.

His voice was hoarse, but I could hear the pleasure in it. We could hardly stand still. We wanted to shout and cheer and dance and hug him, but we stood glued to the ground so we wouldn't break the spell.

*   *   *

After four weeks, ready or not, opening night was upon us.

The audience included the residents who could make it, some of them on crutches or in wheelchairs; the nurses and staff who were on duty; a couple of doctors; some interns; a few locals; and some theater department friends from Smith. Not one family member of anyone in the cast, not one friend of any of the men from outside came. It was a low-key affair. Higher powers wanted this break in the schedule to be as minimal and as controllable as possible.

Just before the performance, Irving, who'd "liberated" a bottle of ketchup from the kitchen, poured it all over himself for blood. He was delighted with his surprise. He'd kept it secret until the last minute. As red drops of ketchup-blood flew here and there, a motley band of men celebrating Independence Day marched along the back of the auditorium, down the aisle, and onto the stage. "Yankee Doodle Dandy" flowed out of them at the top of their lungs. For the opening number, they arranged themselves around the upright piano, a cardboard tree, and a basket of apples.

The Ballad of Johnny Appleseed!" said Fish.

He picked up the basket and started walking through the audience, tossing out apples as the cast sang.

There was a solo from Tom, the tenor, his white hair flying:

Apples sweet and apples sour,
I could eat 'em by the hour.

Bernie, a baritone, sang while biting into his apple

Apple pie and apple tart
Applejack to warm the heart.

Fish, the bass, drew himself up to his full height and sang:
Apple jelly, spice and candy,
Apple cider, apple brandy.

And then the chorus came in:
Some men want money to have and to hold;
To Johnny an apple meant more than gold.

After watching the entrance, I ran to the makeshift changing room to get into my costume, the beaded two-piece, which I was protecting until the last minute. I opened the box where I kept it and saw that the skirt was missing. There was no time to send anyone looking for it or even to tell anybody. There was no one to tell. If I lingered, the butterflies dancing in my stomach would go on without me.

I put on the top, looked in the mirror, and said to myself, "Nobody will notice." A couple of beads fell off and rolled away. I turned around and looked again at my thigh-length tunic. "You can see more at the beach." I jammed the feather in my headband. "I can act the skirt!" And I flew through the corridor to the stage. *Hell, I'm on the wrong side*, I thought. There was no crossover space behind the stage. I could hear Irving saying lines I'd never heard before. He was ad-libbing!

"I wonder where Pocahontas is?"

"Somewhere over yonder, I would expect," said Fish.

Annie was playing a vamp based on "Indian Love Call" to get my attention. There was no time to run downstairs, cross under the stage, and get up to my entrance, so I went on from where I was.

"Here I am!"

The men all had their backs to me as they waited and watched for me to enter from the opposite side of the stage, so there was some confusion and some milling around until, God bless 'em, they rearranged themselves. Only Dave, still in his trainman's hat as he had been from the first day we met him, missed what was happening, but he looked comfortable. He was still singing.

The audience was riveted, not sure what was happening but willing to go along with whatever it might be. Audiences are like that. They stay right with you so long as there's reality. It was very real, what was happening. We didn't know enough to fake anything or pretend everything was going well.

I was having a waking actor's nightmare. This was my family, at least for the moment, no? These were my best friends for the next hour. Why were they all looking at me like I was the crazy one? The hell with them; this was my big scene.

As I barreled on, I sensed a kind of uncertainty, a vibration that hummed among the men, as a red-headed, white Indian in half a costume danced and sang among them.

Even the music sounded tentative. Annie was looking back and forth between me and the vets as if I'd done something wrong and she couldn't understand why.

When I finished my number, there was a huge pause as though someone had missed a cue. The show had stopped, but not in the way I had expected. The audience was too quiet out there.

Yes, something was wrong. They all seemed to be holding their breath. They looked scared.

Then Sam, although it wasn't when we had planned it, stepped forward and sang. His gorgeous Irish tenor wrapped around us like cashmere and silk. His eyes followed the boat that was carrying his boy off to America, probably forever.

But come ye back when summer's in the meadow,
Or when the valley's hushed and white with snow.
It's I'll be here in sunshine or in shadow—
It was the first time Sam had sung the whole song.

The audience would not stop applauding. Sam smiled at them. Irving went over to him and said, "They want you to sing it again, buddy."

Sam sang it again. There was a different kind of quiet now, a stillness in which we could hear the breathing of the audience change to match Sam's. When it was over, they stood up and cheered. Sam broke into a laugh and waved to them.

After the show, I saw Sam speak to Irving, to Alec, and to a couple from the cast who came over to shake his hand. Then he saw me and sent a thumbs-up in my direction. He had a smile that was full of mischief. In my fantasy, *The man I might have married* flashed on a vaudeville card downstage right. *Nice save, Sam.*

The show had flown by. The experience had changed us all. The audience felt it too. They hung around us in front of the stage. They wanted to touch us, shake our hands, prolong the connection, tell us what a good time they'd had. A woman said to me, "I love your outfit."

When I went offstage, Lynn grabbed me. "Why didn't you wear the skirt to your costume?"

"I couldn't find it. It wasn't in the box. There wasn't time——"

"I thought you were gonna be gang-raped to guitar music right there onstage," she said.

"What?"

She was so close to me that her eyes crossed.

"Do you realize what a chance you took out there? A beautiful girl gamboling around half-naked through a group of men who haven't been with a woman, some of them, sweetheart, in maybe twenty years?"

"I guess I wasn't thinking of it like that," I said.

"You better start," Lynn replied. "You could have been scarred for life. My God, I could have lost my grant!"

My legs started shaking.

"Good thing Sam started to sing," I said.

Lynn sighed, one of her big ones, and said wearily, "See if you can find the skirt. I have to return it to wardrobe tomorrow."

She suddenly looked old, at least thirty-five or so.

As I went down the hall to change, Irving came running after me.

"Peggy! Peggy! You forgot your skirt! Here it is. Don't you want it?"

I wanted to throw my arms around him.

"Oh, Irving, where was it?"

"One of the guys took it out of the box you left by the piano during the last rehearsal, when you didn't want to put it on and ruin it before the show. He was playin' a joke on you."

"Lynn is furious!" I said

"She'll get over it. I know her type."

He whistled a couple of bars of "Yankee Doodle" and spoke in a voice somewhere between a rasp and a whisper.

"Are you coming back?" he asked.

"Well, I don't know, Irving. We've got finals coming up and all."

"Yeah. I understand."

He gave me a funny salute like he couldn't find his head for a minute. Then he said, "Oh, there it is." In his finest Durante style, he shuffled off, mumbling, "The Case of the Missing Volley Ball Net. Inka dinka doo, a dinka dee, a dinka doo. Ah doo. Ah doo."

I walked down the hall, thinking about all the men in this building we'd never seen, the ones in the beds and the wheelchairs, those with the missing limbs and eyes and faces. It was suddenly very cold. I ran to the changing room, threw the beaded costume into its box, dressed, and raced back to my future.

The men of the *Johnny Appleseed* production crowded around as Irving, under the night guard's supervision, held the front door of the VA hospital open for us.

"Come back next week," said Fish. "We'll play some volleyball."

There was a chorus of "Oh, yeah!" from the vets.

"You bet," I said, but my throat hurt.

"*A bientôt*, then," from Dee.

"Thanks again," said Biz.

"'Night," said Annie.

Lynn didn't say anything. She was wiping her glasses with a mitten, which caught in one of the hinges.

"Hey, it's snowing!" said Sam. "Geez, I haven't seen snow . . . in a long time.

The Third Degree

When I told my mother that I wanted to be an actress, she was horrified. Mom was a widow by then, and when she consulted her bridge partners about this, their raised eyebrows conveyed their opinions: "fallen woman," "damaged goods," "ruined."

Halfway into the twentieth century, Queen Victoria cast a long shadow. Mom was totally committed to my happiness but worried endlessly about doing the "right thing" according to what would have been my father's wishes.

She made a deal with me: If I earned a college degree that would guarantee me a "real" job, she would support me for the first year of the pursuit of my desire to become an actress. "So long as you have a degree to fall back on," she said.

The idea of "falling back" on anything was appalling to me. To fall at all—back, forward, over, down, out, or in—was equated with humiliation and failure in my mind. I had fallen off a horse twice. I fell down in the old Madison Square Garden four nights in a row while ice skating in front of four thousand people. That's more than sixteen thousand major falls right there, and I was still in my teens.

I chose Smith College because it offered a theater major and Hallie Flanagan Davis, onetime head of the Federal Theatre Project, was dean of the theatre department.

Hallie Flanagan was a groundbreaker. She had led the Federal Theatre, the only national theater our country ever had, during the Depression. She created work for playwrights, actors, directors, designers, artists, and stagehands. She came up with the Living Newspaper form of theater: pageant-style plays drawn from the headlines of the day. Subjects like poverty, housing, and diseases needed attention. *One Third of a Nation* dealt with syphilis in America, a shocking subject at that time that was spoken of only in whispers, but Hallie was fearless. Under the

Works Project Administration umbrella, the Federal Theatre was the only project that earned a profit as long as it existed.

Hallie attracted the attention of the entire nation. Senator Joseph McCarthy of the House Un-American Activities Committee, in his pursuit of celebrities in the arts, wanted her name on his blacklist. When she took the stand during the hearing that ensued, he asked if it was true that she had presented a play called *Dr. Faustus* written by the communist Christopher Marlowe. She replied that Marlowe had been a contemporary and friend of William Shakespeare and had written plays three centuries before Karl Marx was born. McCarthy immediately declared a recess, and Hallie Flanagan was through with him in time for lunch. It was imperative that I take a seminar with this extraordinary woman.

Unfortunately, by the time Hallie got to Smith, she was fighting Parkinson's disease and was not able to teach the three of us in her playwriting class, who had no idea how to write anything at all.

At the end of the term, when we had to hand in some evidence of our work, I was in a state of alarm. I had nothing to show her. I was going to flunk the course. I was saved by a girl in my dorm who suggested a little-known author whom I could "adapt." She'd read his first book of short stories, and said there was one that was practically all dialogue. It was called "My Side of the Matter." I could get it out of the library. It was by a fellow named Truman Capote.

Hallie gave me an A minus. Soon after, she stopped me in the hall outside her office and looked at me curiously. I always felt she could see right through me.

"You know, I've never read that story. I must go over to the library one day and take a peek at it," she said.

I quickly pedaled my bike to the library, grabbed the only copy on the shelf, stuck it inside my jacket, and never looked back.

Truman Capote was at the time sharing his life with an English professor at Smith. That's probably why his book of stories was in the campus library; he had yet to become the talk of New York. I owe this then-stranger a lot. I had never met him, yet, through my college chaos, he reached out to me from the world where I longed to be more than any other. He pulled me through to my graduation as if from prison to a life that had been on hold for the previous sixteen years. The safe deposit box was cracking open.

The last obstacle to getting a degree was the final exam in the History of the Theater from the Greeks to Modern Times, which was also taught by Hallie. Her idea of teaching this course was to hand out a twenty-page reading list and, while we read the books, let us discuss projects we wanted to take on after graduation. I chose "How I Would Start a Community Theater in my Community." I found a book I could copy out of to produce the required paper.

The afternoon before the final exam, Hallie threw out a few trial questions, and it immediately became obvious that none of us had done any of the reading. How could we? We had been lugging furniture around the stage in a production of Franz Kafka's *The Trial*, which featured a male-dominated cast made up of various campus gardeners, associate professors, and a fellow from Amherst. Women were no longer playing men as they had in the previous decade. We were moving the scenery instead.

Smith was the first of the gender-segregated colleges to put men and women onstage together. It was a huge step. There were no more young women dressing up in suits and pasting mustaches and sideburns on their faces. While Harvard clung to its Hasty Pudding shows, we were making history. Yet plays at that time were focused on men, who outnumbered the one or two lucky women onstage with them, as in *The Trial.* So once again, we were trumped. The show must go on, however, and Hallie's reading list never got read. When Hallie grasped this fact, she seemed stunned and ended the last session early with "Well, good luck."

Back in the smoking lounge at Gardner House, where most of the theater majors lived, we gathered in a panic. "What are we gonna do? How are we going to pass this? What the heck is the Commedia del'Arte?" We made such a commotion that Helen Slotnick, a junior who later became a lawyer, approached us and said, "I think I can help you. Wait right here. I need to go up to my room. I'll be right back."

I felt like I was on the Orient Express and someone was about to divulge a major clue to me. In a few minutes, Helen returned with a book she'd used in seventh grade. It was called *History of the Theatre.* Inside, the pages had wide margins. Each century was covered in two pages: one page of print facing a one-page illustration. For example, a picture of an actor in costume for *Hamlet* faced a page of big-print text that was titled, "The Elizabethan Age." We each got a half-hour with the book, and we all earned A's and B's on the exam.

I asked the college registrar to mail my diploma, and it arrived in a nice leather folder. I figured someone else might have use for the folder, maybe as a table mat for a hot plate. I gave it to the Salvation Army. I didn't go to the graduation ceremony, and I didn't say good-bye to Hallie. I headed straight for New York.

Disclaimer:

Sophia Smith founded Smith College for Women in 1871 with the help of her advisor. Single women had male advisors in those days—I know about this because my great-aunt Addie had one—and these men were usually ministers, counselors, or other men of that ilk. My mother had an advisor, a lawyer she couldn't understand, and she'd often make the trip into the city again to clarify what he'd told her in their previous session.

Sophia Smith lucked out. Her advisor gave her a newly invented stereopticon. When she looked through it for the first time, she said, "Why, Reverend Brentlow, 'An Enlarged View of the World.' That will be my motto for the college." Smith became a formidable school and today is coeducational, with a graduate program, a junior year abroad program, and a strong school of social work.

When I was there, Theatre was known as a "gut" course, an "easy A." Every college has them. One of the girls in my class had picked it for her major because she fell asleep in the T's while browsing the catalogue. The college was swarming with women whose goal in those days was to get married as soon as possible after graduation.

There were good teachers at Smith, and very smart students took their courses. Bobbie Fatt was one of them. But even Bobbie Fatt, bright and independent as she was, worried about what people might think of her. The society page of *The New York Times* announced engagements by heading the story with the bride-to-be's last name joined by a hyphen with the groom-to-be's last name. Because of this practice, Bobbie Fatt almost didn't marry Andrew Heine, the man she loved. Well, can you blame her?

Act II: New York

. . . and the Boulevard of Broken Dreams, where there is 'for every broken heart a lightbulb.'

A fair exchange, I thought.

Judith Anderson

"But ah, my foes, and oh, my friends." I saw Judith Anderson in *Medea* on Broadway.

It was 1947. I was fresh from a Greek drama class at college that had left me cold. I had expected to experience the great catharsis around overweening and hubris that I had heard so much about in these dramas. Didn't happen. The professor was beyond dreadful. I sat next to a girl who was using her mother's notes from his class twenty years ago. She even had his exams, with the same multiple-choice questions. The translations read like a road map, and the professor stuttered. Why the Greeks of the day had flocked to the theater, as they did centuries later to see Melina Mercouri in *Never on Sunday,* was beyond me.

Then Judith Anderson and Robinson Jeffers, the poet who adapted Euripides' *Medea* for her, came to Broadway. I sat in the last row of the balcony and was riveted for two hours, along with the rest of the audience. Euripides was the last of the great tragedians and the impetus for modern theater. You might say he moved drama out of the "war and incest" arena and into boy-meets-girl territory. After Jason marries the sorceress, Medea, she helps him capture the Golden Fleece so he can regain his kingdom. Two children later, he falls for a younger woman and tells Medea to get out of town. So Medea sends the new mistress a gown that bursts into flames when she puts it on and burns her alive. After that, she kills Jason's and her children. It's a regular *Daily News,* "see pages 4 and 5 melodrama. Rave.

And I sat there rooting for her. *Medea! Medea! Go, Medea!* I totally got how she could murder four people in two hours. I was right back there with the Greeks in the amphitheater. I had never seen anything like it before, and haven't since. This was the real goods. I felt my psyche shifting inside me. I must have been shaking all the way home because a couple on the 104 bus asked me if I was all right. When I told them I'd just seen *Medea*, they understood immediately. The wife said, "Oh, of course. You'll be all right in a couple of days."

I was thrilled to be joining this astonishing profession. I stood on the beach that summer, an apprentice at Ogunquit, roaring lines from *Medea*, timing them to drive back the ebbing waves, dreaming of my own power, waiting for me to catch up.

Audition

In the fifties and sixties, when an actor went to audition for a Broadway show, a play or a musical, here's how it went.

You took the 104 bus or the Seventh Avenue subway or walked over from a cold-water flat in Hell's Kitchen to the theater district. You entered through the stage door into one of the solid, well-designed, acoustically perfect—sans amplification—intimate, delicious theaters that lined the side streets east and west of Broadway in midtown.

The stage door was usually down a dark alley alongside the theater. It led directly to the dimly lit backstage area, where an ancient doorman in a rumpled uniform and a slouch hat sat in a minuscule office, with mailboxes and a Seth Thomas clock on the wall above his head. He ruled from a desk just big enough to accommodate his solitaire setup. He said, "Yes?" without taking the cigar out of his mouth.

You told him who you were and what time you were expected, and he pointed you to a waiting room with a George Booth lightbulb stuck in a wall socket. You could wait there if you wanted to be with other actors who were trying out for your part, or you could wait in the hall, which was cramped, airless, and lacking windows. Or you could sit on the metal stairs leading up to the dressing rooms or go down into a mold-filled basement where the stagehands hung out when the show was on.

Everybody was nervous. It was a big deal. You had dressed up for the audition. The men wore their best suits, and the women wore high heels they had gotten for free from the union at the A. S. Beck shoe store on Forty-Seventh Street. The shoes were guaranteed to ruin your feet for the rest of your life because of their pointy toes and thin stilts, but they made they your legs look swell and gave you confidence. You wanted to make a good impression with every step. This was Broadway, the Great White Way, and there was a broken heart for every lightbulb on it. And, oh yes, your competition was the cream of the crop.

As it got closer to your turn, as you moved nearer to the wings, to the darkened area just off the stage, you could hear and see the audition of the actor ahead of you. This could be unnerving or reassuring depending on how it was going. Did she get cut off early? Did the director engage the actor in pleasantries? Did the actor have a unique take on the script that had never occurred to you and had made everybody laugh hard and long, even applaud? Should you just go home and clean the oven? And then put your head in it?

No! You've stepped onstage, into another world. Space. Light. You could almost see your script by it. Sometimes the paper shook. Sometimes it didn't. You could never count on anything. You were introduced to a row of people halfway back in the auditorium. You couldn't see them. It was dark out there. Sometimes they would say hello or something friendly like, "So you're going to read for us? Well, go ahead." But mostly they talked among themselves, whispered, laughed, and ate sandwiches.

It was up to you to start or to signal to the stage manager who read with you to begin, depending on who had the first line, and you read a scene from the play that was going to be the liftoff for your future. The stage manager stood downstage from you at an angle, out of the light, with his back to the auditors so they would see only you and every aspect of and flaw of you. He read in a monotone so that you could do all the acting. You couldn't touch him at an appropriate moment as you might in real life, because that would put you in shadow with him. He never moved. You never saw his face, and so nothing could happen between you emotionally that might contribute to your performance. You were as alone as you were ever going to be.

When you finished reading, and shaking, and squinting, you would be thanked—with only a "Thank you"—from the darkness and led away like a dog in a dog show by the stage manager. Or you might be asked to read another scene, to wait and read again after they had eliminated some of the competition, or told to keep the script, which was a good sign because it meant they might call you back another day so they could determine if you were what they wanted, like a new car.

And then you went and had coffee and wondered if there was a lightbulb on Broadway with your name on it.

Today, when it costs a fortune to turn on a lone work light in the theater, auditions are held in office buildings. You get on an elevator with a lot of ordinary people, get out, sign in, wait in a hall, and go into a bare room lit by fluorescents. You read the script or sing the song to three people sitting ten steps away behind a table and in front of a window so you can't see them against the backlight. They're looking at you or not looking at you. It's nice if they look at you, but often they're eating the eternal sandwich and looking at your résumé while you're acting. The reader they've hired to read with you doesn't want to be touched any more than the stage manager did.

So you do the best you can and go for coffee and wonder if there is a lightbulb left over for you.

Falling for Mr. Roberts

Trailer:

At that point, Leigh Gutteridge got on the bus. It was six thirty in the morning, and we had been waiting for him. He had not been to bed, as far as I could see. Clothes askew, hair going every which way, tired, happy, handsome, and lovable, he pulled a woman's sleeve out of his jacket pocket, a long sleeve from an evening dress. He looked at it, puzzled over it, and said, "Where the hell did I get this?" He climbed into the nearest seat and fell into a deep, satisfied, snoring sleep.

That was San Antonio, Texas, where the women went wild over the hunks that Josh Logan had cast for the national road company of Mr. Roberts. *It was the story of thirty-five men doomed to sit out the Second World War in the South Pacific on a freighter, never to see action.*

I had found an agent, Sara Enright, through my college professor. He gave me a note of recommendation to give her. That's how Noel Coward got his start, so I was hopeful.

Sara, her fine white hair piled on top of her head but occasionally straying off in other directions as well, sat in her chair in a narrow, wood-paneled office talking on the phone all day. She never said hello or good-bye on the phone or in person. Waste of time. It was dial, dial, dial . . . "Here, write this down," or "I'm sending so-and-so over to see you." Her door was always open. She was a friend of Josh Logan's from the old days when he, Henry Fonda, and Jimmy Stewart were first starting out and would call on her and sit around her office. She knew everybody and had seen everything. She said to me, "Just remember: There is no loyalty in the theater." I didn't know what to make of that, and I never asked her what she meant by it because I thought it would be prying.

It had been so easy. I'd read five lines for Logan, and he'd said, "Oh, she's fine. Would you dye your hair blonde?"

"Yes," I said, unaware that the experience I was to have would nearly destroy my nervous system.

I called my mother. "Mom, I got a job!"

"That's wonderful. Congratulations! Tell me about it."

"It's in the road company of *Mr. Roberts!*"

"Don't they send road companies out in the fall?"

"I'm going to replace the actress playing the nurse, the only woman in a cast of thirty-five men."

"Why is she leaving?"

"She's pregnant."

I could hear my mom gasp over the phone "Oh, she's married," I said, "to the leading man, and she's going home to have the baby. It's all right."

"It is?" It was a little hard to hear her.

So that was it. I would be making $112.50 a week, of which Sara Enright would get $11.25. With this job, I became a member of Actors' Equity, the union that would protect me from ever being stranded on the road.

I got on a train that wended its way for two and a half days across this beautiful country I'd never seen. I was fascinated by the space of it. Looking out the window from my berth in the middle of the night, with the moon lighting up the prairies, the forests, the amber waves of grain, was the most exciting thing that had ever happened to me. I was working!

When I got to the marble-and-Italian-tile station in LA, the stage manager was waiting for me. He was a stocky guy with curly, dark hair and swarthy, pockmarked skin. He wore thick, black-rimmed glasses that magnified his eyes and a buttoned-up yellow shirt that said "Harrah's" above the pocket.

"That's a nice shirt," I said.

"Yeah, I got it in Reno," he said.

"What are the *hurrahs* for?" I accented the second syllable. "Did you win something?"

"It's a hotel with a casino. It's called Harrah's." He accented the first syllable. He had bad teeth that separated in the middle of the top row. After a long look at me, he said in a nasal voice with a New York accent, "Well, Peggy Pope, I understand you've never done anything. But we'll keep that between us. We won't tell anybody, will we?"

It was a crusher. I didn't like him immediately, and it turned out nobody else did either. His main focus during the tour was furnishing his apartment back home by sneaking hotel furniture onto the scenery trucks. He collected monogrammed towels and washcloths as well, which he asked the wardrobe mistress to sew together into a bathrobe for him.

As a stage manager, he was in charge of directing replacements. He told me where the laughs were in the scene and that I probably wouldn't get them all at first. He also told me about what he remembered hearing during rehearsals in New York, which wasn't much, and of course, the blocking, which, luckily, he had written down.

He was happy when we played musical houses because the union required musicians even if they weren't used. He always ordered twelve bazooka players. A bazooka is a comical horn consisting of two gas pipes and a whiskey funnel that sounds like a kazoo. It didn't matter where we were. We could be in the middle of Kansas, and the players would show up. Quiet and unassuming, they were very nice guys. They hung out in the alley and came into the theater only when it rained. Then they'd go in under the stage and play poker. I thought it would have been great if they'd played music before the show, during the intermission, or maybe around the explosion at the end of the first act. I never suggested it because even I knew the stage manager wouldn't have cared for the extra cues he'd have to give.

Once, during a setup at a new theater, I saw a light fall from the flies (the area where the backdrops are raised up and stored), knocking the hat off a stagehand's head.

"Where is the stage manager?" I asked.

"Out securing towels somewhere," said one of the crew.

The leading lady prefaced her notes on how to play the nurse with: "You'll never be able to do what I'm doing with the part, but here are a few tips." She gave me a list of pauses, poses, and looks that I found intimidating and useless at the same time. I was sure I could do better. "I won't be able to watch you rehearse," she said. "You probably won't be very good, but do my notes and you'll catch on to it."

Horace, the leading man, put her on the train and wept as he saw her off. I ran into him as I was crossing the platform to the train that was loading our company. He stopped in front of me and stared through me as if in a state of shock. Then he went on, and I didn't see him again for the rest of the day. He kept to himself in a private drawing room.

My phone rang the next day.

"It's Horace," he said. "How about coming over, and we can discuss the scene we have together?"

"Aren't we meeting with the stage manager later?"

"Oh, he's not going to help you."

"He isn't?"

"No, but I will. I'm good at it."

"Oh."

"Come by at four," he said. "We can have some lunch here while we talk about it."

"Well, I don't know——"

"Sure you do. We'll run some lines. That'll be a big help to you."

"Oh, I see. Well, okay."

It was broad daylight. What could happen? I'd certainly learn more from him than from the stage manager, and it was nice of him to want to help.

When Horace opened the door, he had an x-ray picture in his hand.

"Look at this. They finally sent it to me."

"What is it?"

"It's an x-ray from when I had my appendix out. I think I'll have it framed." He showed me a white spot on the negative where his appendix used to be.

"Oh, my goodness, you had appendicitis?"

"No. I was going into rehearsal for my first Broadway show. I had the lead, and I thought it would be a good idea."

"Why?"

"Just in case. I didn't want it to burst when I was about to become a star."

"Aha. Well . . . good."

His room was a lot bigger than mine, with a view of the orange trees that perfumed the air everywhere. Years later, when I returned to California, I found that oil wells had replaced them and the air tasted metallic.

Horace wheeled in a luncheon table with a white linen cloth, steak, salad, and rolls on it. He pulled my chair out, and we sat down to eat.

"I like steak," he said. "I have it every day . . . and a vegetable. Very important. Good for you. Protein. How's yours? Okay?"

"Yes," I said, "thank you."

"So tell me about yourself."

"Well, I've been studying at the Berghof School."

"Bergdorf? Bergdorf Goodman has an acting school?"

"No. Herbert Berghof. He's Austrian. He's a wonderful actor, and he has this school—"

"I don't believe in taking classes," he interrupted. "Just get up there and do it. I never took a lesson in my life."

"Really?"

"My first director taught me everything I needed to know. It comes naturally to me."

"Really?" I'd never had filet mignon before, and the salad was full of raisins. It looked like a rabbit had run through it. I wasn't eager to eat it.

"Eat your salad. You need greens," he said.

"Okay." And I did.

When the meal was over, Horace said, "Come over here and make yourself comfortable. I'll run some lines with you." He motioned to the bed.

He propped some pillows against the headboard. I pretended I hadn't noticed. I sat at the foot of the bed and said my first line. Then we discussed how we should shake hands as we met. That led to palm reading.

"You have a very long life line. And an even longer heart line," he said.

"I do?"

"Yes. You're going to break a lot of hearts. I'm worried."

"About what?"

"That you'll break mine. C'mere." He was still holding my hand as he put his other hand on the back of my neck and started to massage it.

"You're very tense. I can fix that."

"How?" I was tense. My shoulders had been aching since I first left home. I couldn't do anything about it.

"I'll show you," he said. "Here. Lie down. I'll give you a massage."

"Uh, I don't think so," I said. "I'm fine." And I thought, *This can't be right. You don't even go swimming until an hour after you eat.* I must have said it out loud.

"Don't be ridiculous," he said. "I just want to help you relax. You'll be amazed how good you'll feel."

"I feel fine."

"And you know what else?"

"What?"

"You'd be a much better actress if you could relax. You're very tense."

"No, thanks. I'll be okay."

"All right. Fine," he said. "Let's kiss and make up."

"We haven't had a fight."

"Is that so?" he said, jumping on me, becoming seriously threatening.

"No! Horace, stop it! Leave me alone! I just had dinner. I'll get a stomach cramp."

"Aw, come on," he said.

"This is impossible! I've got to go now." I jumped up and ran across the room. I was really surprised when he gave up and said, "Okay." He looked at me blankly, as if nothing had happened. "See you at the theater."

Later, I was in my room and heard a knock at the door. I didn't answer. I knew it was Horace. He knocked for a while, and then there was a loud thump on the hall floor. Then there was silence. I waited a long time before I went to the door. On the floor was a package. It contained two bottles of perfume: one was called Danger, the other Surrender.

He was a good-looking, full-of-energy, okay actor. I found him exciting and forbidding. My adolescent hormones were startled to life at his attention. I would spend all day avoiding him. I was so overwhelmed by him that I would start shaking in the wings before my entrance. Then, during the walk across to where Horace/

Mr. Roberts was standing with his chief officer, the shaking would stop. When I got up on the hatch with all the crew watching and had to talk to Horace/Mr. Roberts, looking into his eyes, I would start shaking again. My whole body would do it. I wouldn't know where my next breath was going to come from. It was like being a collapsible paper Halloween skeleton just before the string breaks. Sometimes I would stammer—but maybe I didn't, because nobody ever mentioned it. As I write this, I think his eyes had to remind me of my father's. They were clear and blue and noncommittal. And they gave me a feeling of being loved and left out at the same time.

The scene goes like this: The ship's crew has been studying, through binoculars, two nurses taking showers in their quarters on a nearby hospital ship. Ensign Pulver has invited one of them, me, onboard. I come on and am introduced to the captain. In the course of the small talk between us, the crew gathers, watching closely, until one of them, in a vigorous argument with his buddy, shouts, "I'm telling you, I know! That's the one with the birthmark on her ass!" I look around, and he's pointing at me. The laugh was clocked every night. Sometimes it went on for three minutes. Everyone contributed to it. The exact length of the laugh was recorded in the stage manager's log and sent back to the New York office daily.

It was the most acting anyone in the crew got to do all night, and they seized the opportunity. Each actor had his own personal reaction—a double or triple take, mugging—practiced and kept fresh in front of the mirror during the day. One fellow downstage left managed to let a rolled-up red handkerchief unfurl slowly from his hand at the word *ass*. This is why directors call for brush-up rehearsals, to take out the improvements so the audience doesn't lose track of what the play is about. I think I was shaking through the whole scene.

My life was a nightmare. I had no one to talk to. My understudy wouldn't speak to me, and the wardrobe mistress was a gossip who complained to me when she found greasy handprints on my uniform. The guys were giving me friendly little hugs in the darkness of the wings before I went on. The only other female in the company was a goat named Daisy. I was a mess. My mother's words, "I have every confidence in you," gave me headaches. I was in a jam. I'd never been in a jam before.

I was brought up low Episcopalian, with an easygoing, folksy minister. His name was Dr. White, and he had a head of hair so full and white it would almost blind you as he delivered his sermon in the shaft of light from the church window. My mother had appealed to him, distraught that my father was planning never to attend church with her. Early the next Sunday, Dr. White drove up our driveway, got out of his car, and called to my father, who was digging in the rose garden.

"Dr. Pope, it's Dr. White, and it's time for church!" He then went into the rose garden and had a quiet talk with my father, at the end of which Dad decided he would go to church that Sunday.

So in Kansas—or was it Iowa?—I looked up the Episcopalian church and made an appointment with Reverend Boose. I saw him in his library. It was nice being inside a home instead of a hotel. There was a fire going, a lot of beautifully bound books, a vase of roses, and an Oriental carpet that reminded me of Montclair. A friendly black-and-tan cocker spaniel greeted me and then sat on a cushion to bear witness to my story.

Reverend Boose wore silver-rimmed glasses that reflected the firelight. His hair was thinning. I liked his smile and the fact that he listened to me as if he had all day. I ranted. I raved. I told him about my mother, sitting in a three-story house all alone except for Molly, my dog, who was very old by then. I told him about my dream of becoming an actress, about my need for freedom. I told him I thought I might die onstage one night and have to fall back on my degree after all. That's what they would put on my tombstone: "She fell back on her degree."

"I can feel myself falling, falling. I'm a failure! There's something wrong with me! I wish I were dead!" Suddenly, Reverend Boose jumped out of his chair, grabbed my wrists, and pulled me over to the fireplace. Before I knew it, we were both down on our knees, praying in front of the leaping flames—to remind me of hell, I guess.

"Do you know the Lord's Prayer?" he asked.

"Yes," I said.

"Let's say it together," he said.

When we had finished, he said a prayer on his own in Latin and asked God to "look out for Peggy, one of his children struggling to follow the right path in life. Let her not be led astray by forces around her pulling her in the wrong direction."

He asked me if I would like to add anything or say a prayer myself. Nothing came to me, so we had some tea and cookies and talked about how spring was coming. As I left, he said, "Remember: It's not what happens to you, it's what happens within you that counts."

I had no idea what he was talking about. When I got back home after the tour was over, I wrote him a letter to tell him I had been thinking about him, but it came back unopened and marked "Deceased."

I continued to shake during the play. Finally, I confided in one of the sailors in the cast, one I felt safe with because the only kind of woman he was attracted to romantically had to be plump. He loved plump women. I know this because he told me one day when we were sitting on the bus waiting for the light to change. He saw a beautiful, plump woman waiting on the sidewalk and said, "I wish we were in town for one more day. I'm mad about her." After the light turned green and he knew he would never see her again, he said, "I think my mother was frightened by a Rubens painting when she was carrying me."

I called him up soon after that and asked him to meet me in the hotel coffee shop. I needed to talk. He was a gentle soul who, when I told him my troubles, became quite indignant and said, "That son of a bitch." I asked him, "Tom, can you see me shaking in the scene when I'm on the hatch?"

"Nope. I never noticed," he said.

"I'm shaking so hard sometimes I feel like I'm going to fall over. I'm not tough enough to be an actress!"

Tom didn't respond right away. He considered. He ate some of his toast. He took a sip of coffee. Then he said, "Did you know that human beings are built to fall over?"

"Uh, no."

"Sure. We're built like an inverted triangle: tiny base, getting larger at the shoulder. He took a pencil from his shirt pocket and drew an upside down isosceles triangle on the place mat in front of him. Then he drew it tipping over, added arms and legs to it and my head on its base, hair flying, with a cartoon balloon that said, "Help!" He was sitting opposite me and drew the whole picture upside down. He made me laugh. Then he said, "Did you know that 50 percent of all human endeavors fail?"

"No."

"Abraham Lincoln was defeated at the polls several times and never held public office until he was elected president. Knowing that keeps *me* going."

"I didn't know that," I said.

Then he said, "Would you like me to pretend to be your boyfriend so he'll leave you alone?"

"Oh, Tom, thank you. Thank you very much, but nobody would believe us. I'm way too thin."

I hadn't told Tom that I was attracted to Horace and ashamed of it. I had said all I was able to. His offer and his kindness during that god-awful delayed adolescence I was experiencing helped me to keep going, and gradually I was taken into the cast as one of them. I wasn't a girl to be hit on anymore. Everybody had my number, and I stopped shaking. The trade-off was that, when we went out after the show, women the guys had picked up from town joined us. We'd be sitting around a table, and every time one of these women excused herself to go "freshen up," the guys would all stand up as a courtesy. When I got up to go, nobody moved.

Back in New York, we were booked on the Subway Circuit, a series of vaudeville houses that were offering plays in the Bronx and Brooklyn. Josh Logan came to see us. He sat through the whole performance and came backstage to congratulate us. "What a show. What a great show!" he said. "Unbelievable show! No matter what you do to it, you can't kill it."

"Baptism by fire," said Sara Enright as she squashed her hat onto her head and got ready to go home to the Hotel Gorham on Fifty-Fifth Street.

At twenty-two, I felt burned out. I spent the next several months having trouble breathing and feeling a never-ending fatigue. Finally, I got another job, another chance. I jumped at it.

Madame Modjeska Gives Me the Nod

I was gun-shy after my experience on the road. My knowledge of the world remained shaky. I stammered at auditions when I read for a part. My one credit as the nurse in the fifth and last national company of *Mr. Roberts* didn't impress anybody on the summer stock circuit. I was back auditioning for the same part and not getting it.

"They get their girlfriends," said Sara, my seen-everything agent. "They don't like the idea of someone who's done the part. They want to direct a blank slate."

Am I ever going to work again? I wondered. I spotted an ad in the trades for an ingénue in a play that would tour the Catskills and showed it to Sara.

"Stanley Wolf Players? You want to work for him? He plays hotels. Takes Broadway hits and shortens them to fill the time between dinner and the mambo lesson. Tony Curtis started there. Go ahead. Let me know what happens."

She crumpled up a piece of paper and threw it in the area of her wastebasket. Her dismissal of Stanley Wolf caused me to lose my fear. I went to the audition and got the job.

Stanley Wolf, entrepreneur of the Catskills, produced, cast, and directed eight shows a summer, playing simultaneously. The actors lived together in a mansion provided by Mr. Wolf in Libertyville, New York, and while Mr. Wolf rode around in a puce Cadillac convertible with the top down, we went out on buses every day to play the surrounding hotels. It was my second job on my journey to self-knowledge and freedom, and the play was going so badly that Mrs. Wolf had to lock and guard the doors to prevent the audience from leaving the theatre early.

Stanley Wolf got mad at us.

"You're all sliding around in shit on that stage!" he said. "When you have a funny line, turn front and say it loud. This is a comedy, damn it!"

He replaced the leading man. It worked. The new fellow lifted the play out of the swamp. He was a real actor: older, experienced, and an expert, not like the rest of us novices. When I helped him with his lines, which he learned in two days, I noticed he had silver threads running through his sideburns. He took a shine to me and made me laugh when he told me about himself.

"The neighborhood liquor store always knows how I'm doing," he said. "When I'm flush, I buy champagne. When I'm not, I buy beer. When I'm scraping bottom, I buy their cheapest Gallo wine in the jug."

His name was Phil, and he wore city clothes—a brown jacket and gray pants. He didn't have resort clothes, jeans, or shorts, or the usual summer camp attire we all wore. He didn't even have a bathing suit. He was a grown-up, a man, the real goods. I didn't know exactly what he was doing in our midst. Looking back, I think he must have needed money, was at some crossroads in his life, or was trying to quit drinking. I was too young for these thoughts to occur to me. I simply thought he was a miracle, and I fell madly in love with him. My mom's forebodings were getting smudged in my memory and would soon be erased.

He was magnificent in the play when he took over, despite the lack of rehearsal. Nobody walked out, and Mrs. Wolf was able to get back to riding in the puce Cadillac with Stanley. The playwright had been a bit redundant. On the second night, Phil left out two scenes because the lines he was saying in the first act were repeated in the second. He jumped ahead, right across the intermission, and we got back to the mansion a half-hour early.

We went to the cellar cafe to unwind. It was a bare room with a jukebox and a makeshift wooden bar where beer and Cokes were served. Random tables and chairs left the floor open for dancing later. The only attempt at décor was a poster of Madame Modjeska, the Polish diva, who had immigrated to America in the late 1800s. One of her specialties was that she could sit on a stage and make an audience weep buckets when she read the phone book. In the poster, she wore a low-cut red gown of the same period and sat in the same kind of chair as Grandmother Pope, who had looked down on us from over the fireplace in Montclair.

Madame Modjeska was curvy and lush, with feathers in her red hair and romance blooming on her face. This great Shakespearean actress filled me with awe. She inspired me and conveyed with her pose that she would take up with only the most desirable of men.

Phil spiked his beer with a shot of Wild Turkey from a flask he kept in his jacket. I sat across from him at a small table in the dimly lit room. From the jukebox came Jo Stafford singing an off-key version of *Smoke Gets in Your Eyes.*

"That doesn't sound right," I said.

"She's doing it on purpose," said Phil.

"Oh? How come?"

"It's funny," he said. "Listen. She misses beats too. Or puts too many in. Hear it?"

"Yeah . . ."

"It's a send-up of bad lounge singers in the Midwest. I'm not kidding. I have the record, and there's a picture on the sleeve of two left hands playing the piano."

"Oh," I laughed. "How clever."

"Do you know your eyes have flecks of gold in them?

"Oh, c'mon." Horace flashed in my brain, said *Oh, excuse me,* and made a quick exit.

"It's just beautiful the way they catch the light, green eyes flecked with gold."

On the wall behind Phil, a large roach hiked across Modjeska's bosom.

"Want some bourbon in your beer?" he said.

"Um, no, thanks. This is fine." I wiped the beer rings from the table with a paper napkin. The café was filling up with actors from Mr. Wolf's other shows. Johnny Dayton, the most outgoing member of all the troupes, stopped by our table and said, "Go for it, kids," before he took off after Regina, who was still wearing her Indian makeup and headband. Glasses clinked, an occasional guffaw erupted, and there was Mary Ellen holding forth with anecdotes in her Southern Comfort drawl that promised not to cease before closing. The voices and laughter of the actors rose above the music.

"Don't move," said Phil. "I'll be right back."

Rita had been eyeing Phil from the bar. She tugged at her skintight skirt, which snapped back at her as she started over. When she got to the table, she said, "I'm playing the nurse in *Mr. Roberts*."

"I was in that on the road," I said.

"Oh, yeah? Who was your leading man?"

When I told her, she said, "I slept with him."

"Oh," I said.

We didn't seem to have anything more in common. I watched her as she prowled off and gave myself an aside.

What a vampire. She's stalking my man. I wonder how Madame Modjeska would deal with such insolence.

When Phil returned, he said, "It's hot in here. Shall we go for a walk?"

"But, uh . . .," I said. "Let's be real casual so nobody——"

"But of course."

Outside, he took my hand, and I felt the breeze surf across the goose bumps on my arms and legs. There was no moon, but the stars were out.

"There's the Big Dipper," I said.

"And the North Star."

"Oh, look. Cassiopeia's chair!"

"Hey, shooting star!"

"Where?" As I turned my head to see, my lips ran into his.

"You missed it," he said.

"Oh."

An owl hooted, *"Ooh. Oo."* A dog barked as we snuck across the driveway gravel. A pebble slipped between my sandal and my foot and found a resting place between my toes.

"It's chilly," I said.

"Let's go in the bus," he replied.

"Well——." It was like going into the ocean just before a wave breaks.

"Come on."

We couldn't push the door open, so we had to pry it with our fingers. It creaked as it gave. We got in and felt our way to the back. The seat wheezed as we sat on it. A tear in the leather scratched the backs of my legs.

We talked softly and drank Wild Turkey. I couldn't smell it on his breath anymore, and I was no longer chilly. I hiccuped. I giggled. I breathed and held my breath. He laughed and talked on in a low voice that wrapped around me like the sound of a cello. Before he put his arm around me, he placed the flask on the floor. When I nestled into him, his jacket scratched my cheek. His face felt cool against mine. He kissed me. Outside, a bird called, a mourning dove. I heard a bee buzz behind the seat. The Wild Turkey tipped over and spilled onto the floor.

*   *   *

"What's that glowing?" I asked sometime later.

"Someone's turned on the porch floodlight."

"On us?"

"Looks like," said Phil, peering through the window. "It's the company manager, whatshisname."

"Angus."

"Yeah."

"You think he's going to wait there to see who gets off?" I asked.

"Yup."

"Phil, my mother asked him to look out for me," I said.

"Oh. Sorry, kid."

"What am I gonna do?"

"Tell you what. I'll get off the bus by myself and have a few words with old Angus, tell him I needed some time alone, and after I get him inside, you skin on up to your room."

"And he's going to believe you were rocking this bus all by yourself?"

"Never know till you try, kid."

As I crept up the back stairs of the mansion, I thought about Madame Modjeska, about her beginnings and about mine. *How long is my climb to be?*

When I got to my door, I saw Rita in the hall.

"Where have you been?" she asked.

There was no fooling her. She saw right through me as if I had stolen candy from her. I assumed what I thought would be one of Madame's grander poses, one hand on my bosom, the other on the doorknob.

"Oh, just getting some air," I said. "It was so close in the café, don'cha know?"

I parted my lips and flashed her a smile of forbearance. With a diva's circular wave to her adoring audience, ending with a light stab in the air and a gesture somewhere between "V for Victory" and "Up yours," I was gone.

Marilyn

After she'd finished filming the New York scenes for *The Seven Year Itch*, after her skirt had stopped blowing up around her shoulders as she stood on the grate in front of Bloomingdale's, after "It's a wrap!" was called, Marilyn Monroe would drop in now and then on Lee Strasberg's acting class. Lee was the current guru to the stars, and Marilyn was his biggest catch. It was 1954, and Edward R. Murrow was telling me: "You Are There." I was there.

With a kerchief around her head and no makeup, her skin was even more luminous. It seemed that if I were to touch it, it might evaporate. When she was there, she was the only one in the class who watched the scenes. The lights would go down and a scene would start, and she would watch it while we watched her glowing in the dark with no makeup. How did she do that?

One day, when it came time to leave, I walked out with her. She'd put her kerchief back on, and we were strolling down Broadway when a woman coming toward us stopped abruptly and gasped. Her mouth made an O, and she gasped again. "Aren't you Marilyn Monroe?" she said.

"Oh, gosh," said Marilyn. "You know, people ask me that all the time, and I'm not. I wish I were. I look a little bit like her in certain lights, though." She gave a friendly giggle, and the woman said, "I coulda sworn you were Marilyn." And Marilyn replied, "I'm sorry," and the woman stepped backward as one would for royalty and let her pass.

A lesson in grace, I thought.

In My Merry Widow

So there I was in the out-of-town tryout, at the Walnut Street Theatre in Philadelphia, in a French farce, in a merry widow corset, on my second entrance, in my first Broadway show.

The play, *Moonbirds* by Marcel Aymé, a Frenchman, starred an English actor/knight, Sir Michael Hordern, and a Midwestern sitcom personality, Wally Cox, star of the *Mr. Peepers* TV series. The play had done well in London but it was too parochial for the States and there were whispers of "It hadn't made the crossing." (the Atlantic was much bigger then).

It was November, and it was raining. This was hard on the actors because they had to dress and do their makeup in a separate building and then cross an open driveway to get to the theater. It's the only theater in the world, as far as I know, that doesn't include dressing rooms. It's a theater famous for leaving out space for actors to prepare and participate within its walls. The architect had forgotten to include them in his building plans.

Wind and rain are hard on costumes. They're hard on shoes, hairdos, and morale as well. Dashing through a storm of falling wet leaves just before an entrance doesn't contribute positively to one's performance. It was particularly hard on me when, in my damp merry widow corset and my bare wet shoulders, I was fired between shows that afternoon.

Frank, the stage manager, couldn't have been nicer. He was kind and spoke in a gentle voice when he told me that management was going to let me go. When I screamed "Why?" at him, he spoke even more softly. "They're going to bring in someone tall who won't look so much like you," he said. "Two ingénues in the same play, especially if they resemble each other, are confusing to an audience. It's like bald-headed actors. You don't ever see two of them in a play together." He was trying to make it easy for me.

"*But we're sisters!*" I said. "*Sisters resemble each other!*"

The stage manager turned his empty palms toward me and looked helpless.

"Don't sisters resemble each other?" I said again. He shook his head, shrugged his shoulders, and shuffled off as if they had fired him instead of me.

My replacement, whom they had been rehearsing secretly, was to go on for the final week in Philly. I had actually seen her across the street the day before, walking along laughing and chatting with a member of the cast. I thought she had come down to see him in the play. She'd even waved at me.

The humiliation caused my body to go numb. My head ached as if I were wearing an electrocution cap a size too small. My hands tingled as if to warn me of a heart attack. I sank in slow motion to my knees and then onto my forearms. Then I blacked out and lay sprawled on the cement floor in front of the call-board.

When I came to, I was lying on the union cot in the stage manager's office with a cold compress on my forehead. Frank was staring down at me. He gave me a glass of water and held on to it while I drank so I wouldn't spill it and get everything wet.

He said, "Are you pregnant?"

"Of course not," I said.

"Never been fired before, huh?"

"No."

"Don't worry, kid," he said. "It happens to everybody."

I walked slowly back through the rain, forgetting to protect my merry widow, the costume I was wearing when he fired me after the matinee. The world was ending for me. I had no place in it, no reason to be alive. I was a zero in a void.

The dressing rooms were empty. The rest of the cast had gone to supper. No one had waited for me.

I saw that I'd left my shoes on the dressing table, something you're never supposed to do. It was bad luck, and I had never done it before. I put them on the floor and looked in the mirror. It occurred to me that five actors ahead of me had been fired in the course of rehearsals. The director had been fired. Now the producer had taken over the direction. My thoughts were tumbling over one another, and my gaze drifted down the line of beauty stations to where the other ingénue put on her makeup. Her chair was empty and seemed to be beckoning to me.

After changing into my street clothes, I sloshed across the driveway, kicking the puddles, and reentered the theater. I kept on through the dark auditorium, lit only by a work light onstage. At the back of the house, I knocked on the door of the producer's office.

"Yes, what is it?" he said in his Prussian accent. I opened the door and went in. His glass eye was in his hand, and he was polishing it. He did this often, so it didn't interrupt my concentration. I said, "Mr. Vonner, I noticed today that I am the sixth person you have fired from the show, and I was wondering——. If you were to fire anyone else, it would probably be Beverly Shaw's turn. And if and when you do that, could I try out for her part?"

Mr. Vonner looked at me in a peculiar way, as if he had just been reminded of something he had forgotten to do. After a pause, he said, "I will think about it." He took another pause, put his eye back in its socket, and sighed. "I'll let you know."

I made my debut on Broadway in that show, *Moonbirds*. It ran for two or three nights; I forget which.

The ingénue of my youth doesn't exist today. She was gradually replaced by actresses like Cynthia Nixon and Meryl Streep, women with a sense of of entitlement and smarts, unlike a half a twin from a play running through the rain getting her costume soaked.

*　　　*　　　*

The world didn't end after all. There was so much work around that year, I was soon hired again, this time to replace an actress who had gotten sick out of town.

Viva Madison Avenue starred Buddy Hackett, who took me to dinner as soon as I arrived. We had steaks served so hot that they were still sizzling when they were set in front of us. Buddy told me there was a phonograph under the plate playing sizzle sounds, and when I started to look, he said, "No, no, no! Don't touch it! It'll burn you!"

My joining the cast was so sudden that they didn't have a costume for me. They had told me to bring along a couple of my own dresses, and I had chosen my favorite, a light, white wool dress that I thought would be perfect. I rehearsed with the stage manager, and when I met Buddy for our entrance at the door to the set, he looked at me and said, "Gee. That's a dumb dress. What are you wearing such a dumb dress for? I don't think I ever saw such a dumb dress!" I had just enough time to start feeling bad before we had to go on. He was trying to tell me in his own special way that if you wear white onstage, you attract all the attention and the audience won't notice the star. I guess I knew what I was doing after all.

Buddy didn't like the director, didn't like his notes on the performance of the play, and used to hide from him. He didn't like having to respond "Here!" at roll call. The first day I was there, when we were to meet for notes after the show, he hid behind the high-backed armchair in which I was sitting. I turned to remonstrate with him, and he went "Shh, shh, shh," like a child playing hide-and-seek.

He'd call in sick to avoid rehearsal, and if the director found him, Buddy would pretend he had laryngitis and couldn't talk. When we opened in New York, Buddy got a telegram from a friend that said, "I told you to wait in the car." We closed after the second performance.

However, one learns from every experience. We got rewrites every night in this play, sometimes just before the curtain went up. I learned from Fred Stewart what to do if you go blank onstage and can't remember your lines: Start coughing and pull out a handkerchief. Keep the coughing going into the handkerchief and add some gibberish until something occurs to you to say that sounds like a cue. Any two words will do. Say them and stop talking. Let the other actor get the play back on track. Fred was a genius at this. Actors used to show up early for their entrances to watch him from the wings every night.

*   *   *

The third play I was in that season was *The Long Dream,* adapted from a novel about a lynching in the south. Ketti Frings, the adapter, used to come to rehearsals in a mink coat that trailed along the floor behind her. This play also ran for three or four performances.

I was hired to understudy Barbara Loden. In the course of rehearsals, the producer, Cheryl Crawford, asked me to understudy Isabel Cooley as well. While four black college students in North Carolina were sitting at a Woolworth's lunch counter waiting to be served, our producer was finding ways to avoid paying another salary. She must have thought she could get away with this because Isabel Cooley, a light-skinned black woman, was playing a character who was passing for white in the play.

The first time I saw Lloyd Richards, our director, he faced the stage, put his hands on the front of it—it was as high as his chest—and in one movement jumped up on it, landing on his feet. It was a simple, quiet, dramatic act that took my breath away. He called us all together on the stage to talk about the play. He spoke with passion of the time he was in the Army during WWII, stationed outside Biloxi, Mississippi. He went into town on his first Saturday night there and was literally kicked all the way back to the bus station by a bunch of white men. They told him that if he ever came back into town, they would kill him. "I was stationed there for two years and never once went back into town," he said.

Then he astonished me by saying it would be our job to keep that story in mind during rehearsals, and outside of them as well. He didn't want the blacks making friends with the whites in the cast. I was shocked by this. It was as if I hadn't heard him right. Naïveté is hard to pierce, I was finding. I was a chrysalis concerned only with myself and being on a stage.

Lloyd was ahead of the times. He was a quiet leader who played not just close to the vest but deep inside his skin. This play was about a lynching; it was not just a melodrama. It was life, real and stark. Twenty-four/seven rehearsals were how he planned to get it onstage.

A week later, he asked me to put on black makeup and fill out a gospel choir scene in the play. The more black makeup I put on, the bluer my eyes appeared. It was apparent to the audience, an usher told me, as in "Wha'chu doin' up there in that scene, girl?"

When I told Lloyd about my predicament, he said, "Wear a kerchief and turn upstage." Eventually, he took me out of the scene. I think it was the producer's idea. Lloyd was a patient man and let people make their own discoveries.

I don't know how the black actors felt about my taking a job that should have gone to one of them. Their tolerance of me was a tribute to them, but it was all wrong.

One day, a group of us, disregarding Lloyd's wishes, was standing around discussing where to go for supper during the break, and I said, "I have to run upstairs and take off my makeup." One of the black actors said, "Gee, I wish I could do that." He began rubbing his face like mad as he pretended to clean all the darkness off of it. Then he looked at his hands and said, "It's not workin'," and stood there thinking it over. Not long after that, Clarence Williams III became a major star on TV's *Mod Squad*.

Lloyd became the head of the Eugene O'Neill Playwrights Conference, provided work for many black actors, and discovered the playwright August Wilson, whose plays he directed on Broadway in the years that followed.

*   *   *

All told, I think it was a total of seven nights in three plays on Broadway that season, although Jerry Tallmer of the *Village Voice* researched it and told me it was ten. Whatever. It was a time of living in three different worlds I had never known existed.

July 1954: If Only It Hadn't Been Raining

The night before I eloped, I knew it wouldn't last. I was twenty-five, and it was the fifties. There was a lot of pressure. My brother Jim never got tired of warning me: "A girl can miss her market and end up on the shelf." When he said this, I would picture myself sitting with the soda crackers and the oatmeal on the second shelf in the pantry, in the dim light that crept though the crack of the kitchen door. I didn't want to get married just then, but "missing my market" was a harrowing thought. It brought up a visual of running for a departing ferry boat and jumping for the deck only to realize mid-leap that the boat was coming into the dock instead and that I was going to fall in the water in front of it.

I was still calling my mother in New Jersey every night to tell her that I had gotten home safe when I was really at Joe Allen's or Downey's or out partying. I had to move on, grow up, and get married so I wouldn't have to lie to my mother on the phone at night from an apartment that wasn't where I lived. *What if she called back?* Even though she never did, it was too nerve-wracking.

I married someone extraordinarily inappropriate. I didn't tell anyone. I knew it wasn't going to work. I'm sure a lot of people didn't understand what they were doing back then. It was a time of transition from Margaret Sanger's giving us the diaphragm to therapy's arrival on the scene.

I had met Bill on the third floor of NBC at Rockefeller Center, where actors used the free phones to check their answering services. Anne Meara picked up when I called. She was always great because of the way she'd cheer me on with, "Nothing right now, Peggy," as if the big one was right around the corner, probably coming in as we spoke. She filled me with hope. I'm glad she got out of there. When I run into her now, she always says, "I used to take messages for you," as if some sort of miracle had occurred in her life for which I was responsible.

So I was sitting there in a phone booth, waiting for the surprise summer shower outside to stop, when this fellow came over to me and said, "Hi. How have you been?"

"Fine," I said.

"I haven't seen you since that party."

I couldn't place him. He was "a big lug," an expression I'd heard only in a James Cagney movie, never in life. He was unforgettable, although I couldn't have told you why. My knowledge of men was still pretty flimsy. I just looked up *lug* in the dictionary and found it comes from the Swedish *luggo,* which is something heavy that has to be dragged around.

"What party?" I said.

"The one in the Village."

I'd never been to a party in the Village, but I didn't want to hurt his feelings so I talked to him for a while. We had some mutual friends, and when he offered to drive me home so I wouldn't get wet in the rain, I said, "Okay. Thanks."

He had a beat-up Cadillac convertible whose top didn't work, a kind of oxymoron—a sign, perhaps, of the way that a car reflects its owner's personality. When I sneezed, he said there were Kleenex in the glove compartment, but when I opened it, four hundred dollars worth of traffic tickets fell into my lap. He said he was going to pay them off the following day, but he didn't get the chance. The car was impounded when he came in to get a glass of water at my place. He didn't have the money to get the car out of the impound and was afraid he might be arrested as a scofflaw if he showed up in traffic court without a lawyer, which of course he couldn't afford.

Somehow, I felt responsible. I married him.

Years later, my brother, Jim, reminiscing about Bill, said, "We all liked Bill. There was never a dull moment with him around. He just had that one little flaw."

"What was that?" I said.

Jim, holding himself very still and not looking at me, said in a voice I could barely hear, "Well, he stole."

It was true. Bill did steal. He stole everything from brass salt and pepper shakers to antique furniture. I didn't think of it then, but it occurred to me recently that I'd married the kidnapper who had frightened my parents back in the prologue—a classic case of a self-fulfilling prophecy.

I lived in a world of acting classes, auditions, and theaters. I thought Bill could change. He had energy, dreams, and taste, but no background or credits. He hadn't finished high school, but he'd learned how to survive on his own. His parents had not been there for him, and he had actually made up a father to tell me about—a circus clown who had looked out for him for a while.

I didn't know that people don't change. They get better, or they get worse. When Bill crested and became a smuggler, dipping into dope on the side, he succeeded in convincing an upper-crust Madison Avenue dealer to buy half of an Aztec frieze from Mexico. Bill promised he'd get him the other half on his next trip. Even I knew by then that there never was another half. He was going to get caught soon, get arrested, and go to jail.

I felt paralyzed. Bill always had a cover story, which I always believed. I was the only one who did believe him, but nobody around us ever set me straight. I felt I couldn't abandon him. Abandonment was a deep issue for me. I got over it with Bill.

One day, I came home from a summer stock job, put my suitcase down, and, too tired to unpack, just left it there. Sometime later, Bill said in a voice that sounded odd, gentle for him, forlorn even, "Do you think you could move your suitcase out of the kitchen? Maybe unpack it? It's been sitting there for a year."

I told my friend Cynthia about what I was going through, and she said, "Oh, that happened to me, too. My first marriage, I kept a bag packed with everything I needed for a trip in it. I could pick it up and leave with it anytime, day or night, zip right out the door if things didn't work out."

"What did you do with your toothbrush and lingerie drying in the bathroom?"

"Baggies," she said.

That did it. I'd had enough of being married. I wasn't about to go to jail with him.

Gian Carlo's Bedroom

In the spring of 1960, divorced and free, I saw an ad in the trades for actors to be in a production of *Him* by E. E. Cummings. It would take place at the Festival of Two Worlds in Spoleto, Italy. Cummings was a poet who didn't believe in punctuation or capital letters, but that didn't bother me. I gave one of my best readings for a handsome dreamer of a man called Harry Joe Brown Jr. His name alone inspired trust in me. My name surely inspired the same in him. I was off to Italy, where Gian Carlo Menotti, the head of the festival, awaited me, where a new continent beckoned and a new life would begin. The sordidness of my previous one would be bleached out of existence like a fade-out at the cinema.

There was a whole month before rehearsals: May, the perfect time to see Paris, the Riviera, and Rome. No last-minute deal this, no hop on a train and be there yesterday, as I was used to doing when I got a job. No. A leisurely ocean crossing was in store, complete with deck chairs and stewards swooping over with lap robes and whiskey sours and the captain's table with tinkling laughter rippling around it at something I've said. European society would embrace me, and I would become its darling.

A producer or two might be among them. A film career could open up. There was no limit to the gifts life would hand me on the aptly named Liberty Ship from WWII.

The second night out looked promising. I was invited to a party and immediately felt popular. It took place in a cabin only slightly larger than mine that was filled with a crowd of heavy drinkers. It reminded me of a college frat party in one tenth of the space. I sat down on a bunk with a fellow who seemed pleasant, though somewhat mild-mannered. We talked for a few minutes, until suddenly, he threw himself on top of me. I was wedged under him with my head against the wall, my neck bent at an odd angle that made me feel like it would break any second. Breathing was on hold, and nobody seemed to notice. The man was small but very strong and very determined, and I couldn't budge him off me. *We really don't know each other at all. Is this what you call love at first sight? What on Earth could he be thinking of?* And then—*Is he actually . . . ?*—yes, he was trying to rape me in this crowded, noisy room with some horrible music in the background while nobody paid any attention. It dawned on me that I was powerless under him. I couldn't move any part of myself without him being there ahead of me, blocking a leg or grabbing a wrist. I cried, I screamed, and I shrieked. Nobody could hear me over the din. Or perhaps they thought it was a joke. It wasn't, and it took what seemed like a day and a half to get help that was just inches away. At last, a couple of guys pulled him off, and made him apologize. He didn't seem sure about what he was apologizing for, but I didn't care. I was unable to express myself and was probably in shock—deep fear shock. I went back to my cabin and didn't leave it again until we docked at Le Havre.

Porters and staff formed two lines in the hall and waited outside our doors to collect tips. I marveled at the young girl, my cabin-mate, who had no money—none—and was going to hitchhike to Germany to meet her brother and his wife. Word had gotten around, and they had her number. She hadn't left the waiters in the dining room any tips at all. She put on her backpack, opened the door, thanked them all effusively, handed each one an envelope, and ran off. The envelopes, of course, were sealed and empty. She never knew it, but her courage got me going again. I still think of her now and then. She makes me happy.

My book lay on the table beside the bed in my hotel room: *Paris on $5.00 a Day.* What a ridiculous concept. Whoever heard of linoleum on a hotel floor?

I didn't have a plan. I thought it would all just happen to me. Getting up in the morning and climbing a tower, walking along the Seine and looking at the lovers embracing, going into a church and getting depressed because of all the crucifixes started to make me feel a little creepy, like I was a stranger to myself. I couldn't talk to anybody because, in those days, the French were still busy healing themselves from the German occupation. When I asked directions, nobody understood my Kimberley Day School French. The girl I was then was shy, scared, and naïve, with poor social skills. She is somebody that has a place inside me today, but it's because she has nowhere else to go and I agreed to take care of her.

I went on to Rome and was looking at a poster on a billboard showing where the Theatre Guild tour was playing. A man there was looking at it as well. He was an American.

"Excuse me," he said, "but you remind me so much of an actress I know in New York."

"Really?" I said.

"Yes," he said. "Her name is Peggy Pope."

I couldn't put it together right away. I tried to think whether I knew this Peggy, but I couldn't quite place her. I had become so distanced from myself on account of not talking to anyone for a month that I had forgotten who I was.

Still groping around in my mind, I said vaguely, "I know her."

He looked at me as if he expected something more.

"I mean . . . that's me," I said. "*I'm* Peggy Pope." I was pleased with myself for remembering. It all came back, of course. The man was Stuart Vaughan, who had directed me in a workshop of a play in New York two years before. He looked at me as if I weren't all there. But an explanation from me at the time wasn't going to help. I was far too flustered. So I said, "Well, nice to see you again, Stuart, I have to go. I have an appointment." I could have been the Mad Hatter from Alice in Wonderland.

I probably should have gone to a rest home and recovered from the divorce before I attempted this trip in the first place. However, I was sure that once I got to Spoleto and into rehearsal, I'd be okay.

I managed it. Spoleto is a beautiful, small medieval town in the mountains seventy miles north of Rome. It was a going-back-in-time trip. I stepped into a picture book of narrow streets running between stone buildings, including a church and two theaters, the Teatro Nuovo and the Teatro Piccolo, where we would be performing. The piazza, with its magnificent stairs, was where everyone in our group was supposed to meet, which they did—about three quarters of an hour later than the agreed-upon time. Everyone else knew one another. They were excited about the festival, friendly, and eager to help a lost actress wandering around looking for Gian Carlo Menotti.

"He's home in his house," I was told at the office. "Go over there. You'll find him."

"Don't you think you should call him?" I asked. "Tell him I'm here?"

"Oh, just go on over. He's having lunch. He won't mind."

I found him, the thin, dark, friendly man loved not only for the operas he had composed—*Amahl and the Night Visitors, The Consul, The Medium,* and *The Telephone*—but also for bringing Spoleto to a position of international importance in the musical world. Because of him, Spoleto was blossoming as it recovered from the state of near-poverty in which the Nazis had left it. Who wouldn't love a man who could accomplish all this?

He welcomed me with contagious Italian pleasure, offering me lunch. Then I told him why I was there.

"Ah, but we are not doing that play. The producer did not raise his money."

"But I . . . I bought a one-way ticket. How am I going to get home?" It was all my own fault. It wasn't Menotti's problem in any way, but it was the last straw for me. This adventure was turning into a never-ending debacle. I burst into tears.

In my life I have never met anyone more gracious, more generous, more *Italian* than Gian Carlo.

"Don't worry," he said. "Come into my bedroom. We'll look in my trunk. We'll find a script for you there."

Then it became a conspiracy. He got quiet. He confided in me. "I have interns from America. They will be your acting company, your supporting cast. That way you will have room and board and salary to go home." I had no shame. I followed him into the bedroom.

The setting was simple, full of light. Behind a large bed, he had placed a gilded wooden arch from an old church as a headboard. He had found it lying in an alley behind a church that had recently been restored. The workmen had left it there, discarded, abandoned, forgotten. He was very pleased with himself as he pointed it out to me.

"Isn't it magnificent?" he said.

I dried my tears and made the transition with him. "Oh, my. Yes, indeed."

As we admired it together, I wondered if a priest somewhere was still looking for it.

The trunk was at the foot of the bed, and he shuffled through it. "No, that's no good. No. No. No. Wait a minute . . . no. Ah, here's something," he said. "It's by Jules Feiffer. He's very good. You can do it in the Album Leaves section of the festival. It's perfect. It's short, and to make up for that, you could do a monologue as well. Do you have a monologue? You could get someone to write you one."

Elizabeth Diggs was a writer on the interns list. She wrote me a wonderful monologue for an aerobics instructor with a body tic giving a class. This was very physical.

And since the class spoke only Italian, they thought the body tick was part of the aerobics workout. Every time I did the body tick the audience found it hilarious because they were watching me teaching this class and everyone in the class thought the tic part of the exercise only it wasn't. It was the teacher's body tic. And I would get mad because they weren't doing it right and I have no memory now of how it ended except that it was tremendously funny.

Crawling Arnold by Jules Feiffer was the main piece and a bit of a challenge. It's a hilarious verbal comedy about a family in the fifties with a bomb shelter in its basement. The son, Arnold, is a businessman who refuses to grow up. When he comes home from work, he immediately takes off his jacket and starts crawling around the living room. Shirley Verrett came by from the opera company to play the maid. She had a one-word part. She had to cross the stage from left to right while Arnold's mother asked her, "Where were you today?" And Shirley would answer, "Rioting." What a good sport she was.

I played what Feiffer called a psychiatric social worker who comes in to treat Arnold. And get him to give up crawling and stand up. It was interesting doing a comedy for an all-Italian-speaking audience. They didn't laugh once. It didn't matter. We were having an adventure, and I was its star that summer.

Molto grazie, Gian Carlo.

Joe Papp Goes Public

A Brush with Shakespeare

Joe Papp was a slight man with dark hair, dark eyes, and a soft voice, a man of courage with a passion for Shakespeare, a sort of DuPont of the people. Remember "Better things for better living through chemistry"? His motto was "Better living for better people through Shakespeare."

I didn't know Joe Papp well, but I worked for him on a school tour of *Twelfth Night,* playing Maria. I had been calling him for eight years to get a job. You could do that in those days. You could call a producer directly, sometimes even get him on the phone or leave a message for him, knowing he'd return it. It was a smaller world then, more personal, less bureaucratic. Today, with more people, there's less humanity.

Twelfth Night was a tour of public schools in the Bronx, Brooklyn, and Queens. We performed at ten in the morning at each school. I didn't care. It was thrilling to be playing Shakespeare for Joe Papp at whatever time he decided. It was a good company that included Charles Durning, Mitch Ryan, and Karen Black.

Joe Papp's idea of directing was interesting. His solution for the comedy scenes was to cut everything that didn't work the first time we did it. Although alarming to the actors at the beginning, this approach turned out to be a good thing. A lot of the humor involved puns and topical references from Shakespeare's time. The audience would have needed footnotes in the nonexistent program.

One day during rehearsals, Joe called a special meeting to say he was sending a telegram to the federal government to protest the treatment of Judith Malina and Julien Beck of the Living Theatre. When the IRS come to collect back taxes and close them down, Malina and Beck had climbed out the back window and become fugitives. Joe said we should all sign the telegram and that it was going out at five o'clock the next evening.

Let me say up front that the McCarthy years scared me. I had watched him on TV and worked with actors who had been blacklisted and were in weakened health and spirit owing to his persecution. Having met actors whose lives had been destroyed by the blacklist, even to the point of dying before their time from the stress of it, I was haunted and insecure, worried about becoming blacklisted myself if I signed something Joe Papp dreamed up. *The government has pretty much established its right to collect taxes,* I thought. How they did it was questionable, and it scared me to think that they'd come after me for protesting such treatment of a tiny, out-at-the-elbow, avant garde theater downtown. I didn't want to sign something that would get me in trouble with the federal government. I had no idea what the Living Theatre's productions were about; they didn't make any sense to me. *Leave me alone,* I thought. *Just let me act.*

Joe, on the other hand, had survived the blacklist of the fifties. Fired from his job and left to his own resources, he had founded the New York Shakespeare Festival, "a free theater" on a little outdoor stage on the East River. This quickly grew into quarters on Astor Place, for which he paid the city a dollar a year. He had built six stages in this old white elephant, producing plays by authors living and dead, known and unknown. Some of the plays moved to Broadway and to film. A major cultural force, it is called the Public Theater today.

I also didn't have his strength, brains, or business acumen. I didn't want to be told what to do politically, even by Joe Papp.

As Tennessee Williams might have commented, "Self, self, self. That's all you ever think of, honey."

Right. True. But I had also grown up hearing, "Don't sign anything until you've read the fine print." Five o'clock came and went, and I didn't sign the telegram. Nothing more was said about it, although Joe Papp didn't hire me again.

Rehearsals continued. We got to the technical and dress rehearsal, which is always a nightmare because you get the lights, sound, and props for the first time. I also got a fifty-pound costume, which of course made me forget all my lines. At one point, I had difficulty balancing four long-stemmed goblets, each a foot high, on a small, round tray as I kicked my dragging dress around at every turn, looking for my exit door.

The set was merely a suggestion, so it could travel easily from school to school; it included three slender arches to indicate the doors, easy to shift around for scene changes, and no furniture. However, the doors all looked alike, and I got confused with my tall goblets teetering and my lurching costume attacking me. It was the only time in the theater that I've ever felt really alone. It was my exit, and I couldn't find my arch. There was the dead sound of complete quiet around me. There was no one to talk to and nothing to say. I had said everything. I could say something else, but that wasn't going to solve my problem.

Had everybody gone to lunch? Was there a fire drill taking place? Finally, I stopped dithering about and called out to the gods of tech rehearsal, "I don't know where to go!"

A calm, dryly amused voice from the depths of the auditorium came back with, "Why don't you just . . . go home?" It was Joe Papp. For the briefest of moments, the idea flickered in my mind. *Does he mean it? Should I have signed the telegram?* Then I decided, *No. He's hilarious. He's a hilarious sadist. He's been sitting there the whole time, enjoying my predicament.* Relaxed, laughing, and loving that kind of humor, I found the right door and got out of there.

Just as we were getting used to performing on a bare stage at ten o'clock in the morning and discovering the truth that all an actor needs to perform is "two boards and a passion," I noticed something odd. The ingénue was making her entrance later and later, until it became necessary for me to lace her into her costume onstage during the performance. She was coming on half-dressed.

There's a certain kind of actress who just has trouble keeping her clothes on.

So I'm lacing up Olivia, saying my lines into her back while she shakes her hair in my face and wiggles her hips as the scene starts. Viola, disguised as a boy, delivers a love message from Orsino to Olivia. Olivia, who is attracted to Viola, thinking her a handsome fellow and wanting to know more about him, says, "You might do well. What is your parentage?" To which Viola responds, carefully so as not to give the game away, "Above my fortunes yet my state is well. I am a gentleman."

One particular day at this point, a boy in the audience shouted out in total disbelief, "Oh, yeah? Show us your cock!" And this was only Act II.

It was deadly quiet for about seven seconds, and then the girls started to crack up, first Olivia and then Viola. Then there was pandemonium in the auditorium. Finally, the principal barged into the room and everybody quieted down. He stayed to see the rest of the play, but that scene was damaged forever. The cast would watch from backstage and take bets on who would laugh first at the memory of the debacle.

We ran into some really tough audiences toward the end of the run of *Twelfth Night.* We were all getting weary. Falling out of bed at six o'clock in the morning to frolic around in a Shakespeare comedy at ten was turning into a kind of Chinese water torture. It was a wet November, undecided on whether to snow or rain or give the sun one last chance. We were schlepping out to the boroughs to perform for these hooligans who had to be guarded by monitors in the aisles. One day I was doing a scene with Charlie Durning, who was playing Feste the clown. He was singing, "O mistress mine, where are you roaming?" when I felt a sharp pinprick on the side of my neck, then another on my hand, then others that made a *ping* sound on different parts of my costume before the tiny pieces of metal bounced onto the stage, sounding like rain falling.

Joe Papp felt it was important to show kids in outlying schools, who had never been to a play, what it was like to see one. Their only frame of reference was, perhaps, a shooting gallery at a carnival—sitting ducks. The boys brought paper clips with them, which they opened up into V's and sent flying, powered by elastic bands. They didn't throw tomatoes. They shot us.

I was furious. I wanted to scream at them, "My face is my fortune!" Instead I turned upstage under the storm of paper clips and special-delivered my lines to the back wall.

Not Charlie Durning. Awarded the Silver Star in WWII, he was already carrying a half-pound of shrapnel around in his body. A few paper clips couldn't faze him. He took a hit just below his eye that could have blinded him, but the war hero never flinched. He kept right on playing his lute and singing his song: "Journeys end in lovers' meeting/Every wise man's son doth know."

Afterward, during the talkback, Charlie answered a question addressed to him,

"What is the time of this play?", by saying, "About two hours." He cracked me up. I've known Charlie Durning since he was making the rounds to get work, teaching dancing at Arthur Murray's for a living and playing a cherub in a church play on weekends. I've always loved him, as I imagine everybody else has.

We were to play until Thanksgiving, but on November 22, while the kids were shooting paper clips at us, someone else was shooting President John F. Kennedy in Texas. The cast was told quietly backstage that he might die but that we were to continue to the end of the play, as there was fear of what might happen if we stopped in the middle. The school staff wanted to get everybody out of the auditorium and back into their classrooms in an orderly manner before they announced the news to the students. Viola, the woman disinclined to wear clothes, lost it. She started to become hysterical, until somebody slapped her. I have a memory of the thought passing through my mind that she had always wanted to be Marilyn Monroe, and the idea that she might never get to sleep with Kennedy was too much for her.

I did the unforgivable some years later, cornering Joe Papp during an intermission in his theater and saying, "Mr. Papp, I called you for eight years before you gave me a job. Am I going to have to call you for another—" He interrupted me pleasantly with, "Do you realize how many people call me for more years than that—their whole lives, sometimes—and still don't work for me?" You don't corner Joe Papp. I decided to take it as a compliment and felt lucky.

On the other hand, *Twelfth Night* is the setting for all my actor's nightmares, in which I don't know my lines or where my costume is, don't have time to make my entrances, don't know where to go, and don't have a friend to reach out to for help.

Hey, easy come, easy go. It's a tiny price to pay. Minuscule.

Heroes

I met Elaine Stritch on *Trials of O'Brien*, an early sixties New York TV show starring Peter Falk. Well, I sort of met her. She was pointed out to me. Nobody told Peter Falk who I was either, which was perhaps just as well. I would probably have looked him in his bad eye and gotten off on the wrong foot. Nobody was actually introduced on that show. My guess is that it was a new show. TV shows of this kind were usually done in LA, so there was a lot riding on its being a success and attracting more TV series to the East Coast. There was much to do and little time. Introductions were not high on the list.

I was excited and frightened, as was my wont. I was in the unknown, in which the questions *Will I do well? Will I get it right? Will I mess up?* hovered around me like dragonflies. I had the job, didn't I? I was only there for the day. They didn't have time to fire me. Of course, they could fire me whenever they wanted to, but luckily, I didn't know that at the time.

A striking blonde was pacing back and forth in a cocky way on the set, which was the wide hallway of a hospital with lots of people moving purposefully here and there. It was Elaine, a regular on the series. I didn't know anything more about her than that she belonged. In the midst of her striding and my wandering, our paths crossed. Neither of us stopped, but as we grazed each other's territory, Elaine growled out of the side of her mouth in my direction, "Everybody's scared." She only had to say it once. I looked around the set and fantasized everyone shaking with terror. I felt better. It's a great thing to learn——one of life's sweet, shocking facts.

Our paths have crossed again over the years, and Elaine always stops to talk now. I particularly like the story she tells in her one-woman show about the actor who quit drinking. For years, he stood in the wings before his entrance with a glass of booze, which he would then bring onstage with him. Finally, he stopped cold turkey. When he called it to the attention of an old drinking buddy, his buddy said, "You goin' on *alone?*"

Barbara Cook, whom I've known since the fifties, sat next to me at Christmas dinner a few years ago and said, "You know, Peggy, I'm seventy-two now, and for the first time in my life, I feel really comfortable with myself."

The Swedish filmmaker Ingmar Bergman writes in his book that he woke up at four o'clock every morning of his life scared. But he always got up and went to work. Liv Ullmann, his wife, says in her book that when he had a nightmare, he would wake her up to tell her about it. She always listened because she knew she would be in a film about it the next year.

In the sixties, Arlene Francis, who starred on the TV show *What's My Line?*, had to deal with various accidents in her life, including in the same year a flowerpot that fell off her windowsill and killed a stranger walking by underneath and her chauffeur's running over a pedestrian. Neither accident involved Miss Francis personally, but it was still a pretty bad year for her since she was a celebrity and the newspapers covered these events like drooling jackals.

I was once in a car with Woody Allen, driving to the Catskills to see an improv group in which a mutual friend was appearing. He had been invited to serve as the emcee on *What's My Line?* and introduce Arlene Francis. He mentioned his current nightmare was that he would refer to her as "Arlene Francis, that famous murderess." But he didn't, and in fact she wasn't, so it all went well.

Roscoe Lee Browne, the golden-voiced Jamaican actor, helped me out in rehearsal one day when my work was a shambles, my life wasn't going well, and my relationship with the director was definitely off. I was in deep trouble all around. On a break, I went over to Roscoe and addressed him as the exemplar of wisdom that I thought he was.

"Roscoe, what do *you* do with your demons?"

He paused. "I invite them in," he said, "and offer them tea."

Maureen

I was still in high school when I saw Maureen Stapleton in her Broadway debut in Tennessee Williams's *The Rose Tattoo*. Twenty years later, I was in the revival with her. She got two separate rounds of applause on her first entrance. Fresh out of rehab—she called it "the funny farm"—she got a hand for being there in the first place. Then there would be a pause as the audience realized that she had lost sixty pounds since they had last seen her, and she was looking sexy as hell moving around on that stage in a white slip. They applauded her again for that *every single night.*

I watched her every night from the wings. How did she do it? I didn't have a clue. Her performance poured out of her spontaneously each time; it was real, full of magnetism, and always new. At the bows, before they knew what they were doing, the audience rose together and cheered. Today this is a routine formality, but back then it was rare. Audiences did it only when they were moved by greatness.

During rehearsal, when I would ask some question of the director, Maureen would burst in with, "Don't think, Peggy! Don't think! Just say the words!" Now I know what that means. Then, I was still trying to figure out everything in my head. I believe Maureen started out spontaneous, or got there very quickly. She was an amazing actress with a heaping measure of passion.

I thought it odd that she needed the stage manager to walk her to the wings every night of the run. She was afraid to go onstage. She was afraid to fly in a plane, which made a film career difficult. I believe her life was one confrontation after another with deep fear. But once in the fray, spontaneity was her armor and friend, and with a quick joke, she was off to battle.

We played the Billy Rose Theatre, which was just around the corner from Times Square. On New Year's Eve, the limo that called for Maureen every night failed to arrive. When she came out and it wasn't there, she sat down on the curb in her fur coat and started swearing a blue streak. It was a natural thing to do. You do two shows, you're onstage the whole day, and you come out to find no limo.

"#s#%/#x*+##%x* *" she said.

I hung around and watched for the car, and when it seemed a hopeless thing, I approached a cab and asked the driver to help. He was taking a couple to the Port Authority two blocks away. I asked if they would be good enough to share the next two blocks with the "First Lady of the American Theater" so she could then take the cab home. They agreed somewhat reluctantly. The cabbie said, "So where is she?"

"Oh, she's right over there," I said as I pointed to what by then looked like a bag lady in a beat-up fur coat sitting on a curb next to a couple of paper bags, cussing in high dudgeon.

The taxi group became totally quiet and went into shocked-stare mode. I rushed over to get Maureen and her secretary. They squeezed into the cab and were off before there was a chance for a change of mind.

As the cab drew away, the limo pulled up. What to do? "Why don't we take it up to O'Neill's?" suggested my friend John, who had been watching the scene. "It's been paid for."

And that, I confess, dear reader, is what we did—and, may I add, some bystanders applauded.

I think if Maureen had seen this, she would have roared, "That's it, Peggy! That's the idea!"

Intimacy

I won a prize for acting long ago when the Obies were given out at the Village Gate, a theater on Bleecker Street. It was summer, and I was wearing a white dress, sitting at a bare table with the cast of the play in which I was appearing. We were having hamburgers, salad, and beer. The prize was for Distinguished Acting in an Off-Broadway Show. The show was called *Muzeeka* by John Guare. When my name was announced, I felt my face go out of control, moving every which way at once. It had a mind of its own, seeming not to be a part of me at all yet staying attached to my head, carrying on in a disjointed dance for a while before it finally calmed down. It really alarmed me. I didn't want anyone to see this and didn't know what it meant. It has just occurred to me now, as I'm writing this, that I was way too shy to win a prize, to be singled out as a winner. And it was my face, feeling cornered, that struggled to tell me this. Luckily, the rest of me stayed in the room.

In the show, I played a hooker in the Village who specialized in Chinese basket jobs. Okay, the Chinese basket job is the ultimate form of impersonal sex, sort of a reverse kama sutra. It involves a basket big enough to accommodate a woman sitting cross-legged in it. There is a hole cut in the center of the basket, and the woman sits over it. The man lies underneath while the basket and woman spin slowly around on top of him. They have sex through the basket and don't ever have to touch each other in any other way.

In *Muzeeka*, we had a low budget for sets, so we had to stylize everything. We used a double-decker bed from St. Vincent de Paul's thrift shop. A flat piece of wood suggested the basket and hung from the bottom of the upper bunk. An actor doubling as a kabuki stagehand did the turning as I lay on my stomach eating an apple and delivering a monologue to the audience about Martha Raye and Vietnam while Sam Waterston had an orgasm. We never touched at all.

The hooker had printed cards that said:

EVELYN LANDIS
CHINESE BASKET JOB, YOU LIKE?
With a phone number here

Guare had seen this message in graffiti on the wall of a phone booth at Sixth Avenue and Waverly Place, and it inspired him to write a play about Vietnam.

I would hand out these cards to audience members during my exit up the aisle, but Sally Ordway got pretty pissed off because it was her phone number on the card. It was just a joke, but nobody remembered to change it when Samuel French published the play. I ran into Sally recently. She's an old lady now, and she's still fuming about it.

When my name was called and my face started leaping around, I got up to get the award but then sat down again and asked our director, Melvin: "Was that my name they said?" He said, "Yes! Get up there, bitch!" So I went to the front of the room and said, "Thank you, thank you, thank you, thank you, thank you, thank you, thank you!" and gave Estelle Parsons, who was handing out the award, a big hug that made her wince. Someone told me later that she didn't like to be touched, but she's in a funny business if that's true.

Intimacy—it's tricky.

Dave

There was a character named Dave who used to plant himself outside Sardi's. He wore a brown jacket that wouldn't stay buttoned, and he would call out in a rust-coated voice to people going in for lunch or dinner, "Who are you? Are you anyone?"

Celia, his sometime buddy, clutching her shopping bags, would shout, "Forget him! He's nobody!"

Dave found out who everybody was. He called me Miss Pope and asked for my autograph every time he saw me. Once he asked me if I'd get him James Caan's autograph the next time I went out to the coast.

"It's a hard one to get, and I really need it," he said. 'I'd go out there myself, but I can't get away just now."

He always had two or three copies of *Players Guide* with him, each one with pictures of about two thousand actors in it. When I asked him why he needed more than one guide, he said, "Those are my backups!"

Everybody who worked in the theater district knew Dave. He was even written up in *The New Yorker* once. The reporter followed him around for about two hours. The only celebrity spotted during that time was me, but they put it in "Goings On About Town" anyway.

Dave had a job at a dairy in Astoria, but when I saw him a few years ago, he told me he didn't work there anymore. The last time I saw him, he'd aged and was looking like the guys at the OTB on Seventy-Second Street—seedy, shabby, unshaven. I had tried to duck him, but he saw me and started calling, "Miss Pope! Miss Pope! I need to ask you something!" So I stopped. He didn't have his

Players Guides with him. He came over and said, "Miss Pope, could you lend me a quarter?"

Then I never saw him again.

Ann Miller

Acting with Ann Miller was like being in a Woody Allen movie where the lead character steps out of the frame and starts performing in the midst of strangers. A living piece of celluloid accustomed to acting only when the camera was on her, she stood or sat politely, her whole body totally still, expressing nothing while I said my lines. Then she'd burst into glorious song and dance. It was the closest I ever came to being in a Busby Berkeley musical.

I had the opportunity of making her wince once or twice during the song I sang to her. There was a high B flat in it, which I couldn't always find when I wanted to. Ann's eyes would go crazy at that. The wince was minimal and involuntary; the rest of her never moved. It was her long, thick, fake eyelashes that betrayed her. They fluttered up and down like the shutter on a camera when the film runs out. As I persisted in pursuing my fleeing note, I would see tiny chips of celluloid reflecting the light as they flew off of her. She was a good sport, however, and never commented on my faulty singing. She seemed to like me and trust me as the principal player that I actually was.

At that time, I was frightened of singing. I had no idea how one got all the pitches straight, especially in a song of two and a half octaves. I actually had a good ear and a sense of musicality, but if I got too frightened, I'd hold my breath and go deaf and sing any old thing. When the heavyset character woman with the big voice in the ensemble said, "Why don'cha let me sing your songs for you from the wings and you could lip-synch 'em?", I knew I was in some real trouble. I was saved when a young girl in braids and braces from the crew came up to me and said her father was a hypnotist and had helped a few singers with this problem.

I said, "Take me to him."

He had a machine with a spiral maze inked on it. When he turned it on, the maze spun around and I went straight under as he talked to me in a soft, confident voice. "Relax, relax, relax. You are going into a light sleep now. You will remember everything I say, and when you wake up feeling refreshed, you will no longer be frightened. You will know that you can sing perfectly, with every note on pitch." He kept on talking like that. The only thing I wasn't aware of was time. I don't know how long it took for him to convince me of what he was telling me, but I doubt it took any longer than it takes a stage magician. The man *was* a real magician. That night and for the rest of the run, I sang just fine. I will always be grateful to Ann Miller and her beautiful eyelashes.

She didn't seem to have any fear at all. She had been hired to take over the role of *Mame* on Broadway, having never been on a live stage with lines before. "Never mind," said the producers, who got a second company together for her to practice with down in Florida. In six weeks and five wigs, she was not just talking but singing, dancing, acting, and fast-changing. She did it—just did it! She was a phenomenon. She sweated a lot and made good use of the five wigs, which got changed between dances. Her only questions involved technical aspects. One day, she said, "Tell me, Peggy, what are the flies?" I told her it was the area above the stage where they "flew" the sets up out of view when they weren't being used. She looked up into the darkness, said, "Oh, my," and decided she didn't really need to know that. I decided not to tell her about lights and things falling down from them, and we went on with rehearsal.

She asked Phillip, the stage manager, if they could lay down a tap board for her thirty-two-taps-a-second dance in the first act. He said, "Well, it would require stagehands coming on in the middle of the scene to do that. It would take the momentum out of things."

She said, "Oh, my friend Eleanor Powell's a got a small tap board in her garage. I could ask her to send it to me."

"Miss Miller," the stage manager said, "it would take at least a half-hour no matter what the size, and the union would be hard-pressed to do it without going into overtime." Although she was very disappointed, she was a good sport about that too.

Ann never did understand curtain calls in those days of pulleys and hand-pulled curtains. Our theater's curtain had a twenty-pound iron bar in its hem to make it fall fast, and it was important not to be in the way when it came down. The stage manager was in charge of giving the curtain puller the cue to raise and bring down this monster. The drill was as follows: curtain goes up; we all bow; featured players step forward, bow, and step back; Ann Miller, the last to go, steps forward, bows, steps back; curtain falls; nobody's decapitated.

To look out at the audience in Fort Lauderdale was to behold a sea of white hair, which rose up immediately at the end of the show, each whitecap heading for its own limo as fast as possible. At the very first curtain call, what we saw was an audience already on its feet. Ann, excited by what she thought was a standing ovation, stepped out under the descending curtain to take another bow, totally forgetting to wait for Phil's cue. Harry, the curtain puller, had to jump up and throw his entire weight onto the rope of the half-descended curtain about to slam onto the star's head and kill her. This kept happening as we kept getting more and more "standing ovations." One day Ann cried out, "Eighteen! We had eighteen curtain calls! Isn't that something!" She didn't notice that her huge black wig was askew. Harry had been a fraction late. She never realized as we walked offstage that day that Harry was being carried away in an ambulance with a serious hernia.

In my role as Agnes Gooch, I was inspired by Mame's stirring speech, in which she said, "Life's a banquet and most poor sons-of-bitches are starving to death! You've got to go out there and live! Live! Live!" So Agnes follows her advice. About eight and a half months later, she comes back hugely pregnant to ask in song, "What do I do now?"

The stage had been redecorated in a Japanese vein. The only furniture was a very, very low bench. When Mame tells me to sit down, it's a funny sight gag. Trying to balance my great stomach as I bend my knees, reaching behind me, sinking ever more slowly down, down, down. I finally hit home plate. It had occurred to me during rehearsal that it would be even funnier if I missed the bench altogether. However, I couldn't seem to manage it. I kept thinking about it and working on it, and finally, about three weeks into the run, I ended up on the floor, really surprising myself. I was right. It was so funny that even the musicians in the pit cracked up, and the show sort of came to a halt because the audience couldn't stop laughing. I was laughing, and Ann couldn't say her next line. It was very hard for her, as she was religious about keeping still while another actor was acting. I hadn't thought about that, and I ask her forgiveness now, late as it is.

I know she called Peg Murray, the actress playing her co-star, in the middle of the night and, without saying hello, started right in with, "Is she going to do that again?" Peg, the soul of wisdom, told her not to worry and to just mention it to the stage manager.

I only did it that once.

Jimmy Stewart

When we met to begin rehearsals for *Harvey* on Broadway, the 1970 revival of the play about the rabbit, we were told that Mr. Stewart would not be there for the first week. He was playing golf with President Nixon at that time. However, we weren't to be concerned; he had played Elwood P. Dowd in the movies and knew all his lines.

When Jimmy Stewart walked in the next week, he was every bit the dream that preceded him, no question. He was the real goods. I had never been onstage with anyone so real.

In my scene with him, he invited me to meet him later at a cocktail party. At our first rehearsal, I used my own purse when searching for a piece of paper so I could write down the address. I was sitting down and had an impulse to look up at him, and I saw this tower of a man, this living icon, peering into my purse with me. I had a sensation: *He knows all about me, just by looking in my purse. Everything.*

I wished I had a nicer bag. It was just a beat-up, everyday purse. *What was in there?* I wondered later. I felt I'd better check. Aside from the usual wallet, keys, and appointment book, there were breath mints, a comb, a small Mason Pearson hairbrush from England, lipstick, liner and lint, dental floss, part of a muffin, Kleenex, diaphragm . . . *oh, dear me.*

"I'd like to give you my card," he said. That was actually his next line. He was so smooth. All I had to say was, "Oh, thank you."

On opening night, with mounted police at the stage door holding back the crowds, I was fully aware of what a big deal this was. I was so nervous that I didn't think I'd be able to get through the scene with Jimmy. When it came time for him to give me his card, I dropped it. On opening night! I dropped a prop, a *pivotal* plot prop. I couldn't move.

Jimmy Stewart just picked it up as if that were part of the scene, and I immediately dropped it again. I was wearing white gloves, and they made me fumble. Jimmy picked the card up again, and this time I opened my purse; he put it right in there and winked at me. The next day, the critic for the *Times* mentioned what a nice moment it was.

Every night after that, when I went down for our scene, he would be hiding in the curtains, waiting for me. When I got close, he'd part the curtains and say very quietly, "Boo."

Psychology of an Enchanted Evening

Just as I entered a party, a man came directly across the room to me. He said hello, smiled, and offered to get me a drink. The lyric "Across a crowded room, you will meet a stranger" came into my head, and I wondered why I had thought it so unbelievably corny when I first heard it.

While I was humming along, appreciating how life imitated art, he went for the drink and left me wondering if he was the reason I had gone there that night instead of finishing the John Irving book I was so into. He was back before I had a chance to think further and spent the next ten minutes by my side as we assessed the assembled guests and agreed that we were the only interesting people there. When he said, "Let's get out of here," I, with wobbling knees and thumping heart, followed him down to the street and into a cab, in which we started on the road to passion.

He was short, I discovered, and some kind of boring CPA. But my shrink had asked, "What are the qualities you want in a man?" I had said, "I want tall, dark, exciting, funny, smart, successful, in the arts, an architect, maybe, um . . . witty—"

He interrupted me. "How about a nice, gentle man?" Spraying ice water on my hot fantasy, he said in an unusually gentle fashion, "Go out with him three times before you close the door on him."

The second time that Juan Enchanted Evening and I had dinner together, he was still boring and short. He didn't seem to have anything to say. I had to do all the talking. The third time, he said, "Do you know your eyes are green but they're flecked with gold?"

I did know this. "Excuse me," I said, "I'll be right back."

At the pay phone in the hallway to the bathroom, I called my shrink and said, "It's been three times. Is it okay to go to bed with him now?"

My shrink said, "These things have their own way of developing and, uh, we need to talk about it but, uh . . . I'm in the middle of a session here, and, uh, can you wait until next week, when we're scheduled to see each other?"

Well, I couldn't wait. What if this suddenly great guy lost interest while I was waiting around for some dumb shrink's permission? I knew what I wanted. So I went ahead, and it turned out that I really, really loved him in bed and the most extraordinary things happened there, things that probably happened to the people in the crowded-room song.

Then I found out the lad was married, and I'd done it again. *Why? How?*

I didn't get it.

The shrink said, "Don't you see? It's easy. A married man is a marked man. You can spot him at a glance. He's more comfortable with himself; he's relaxed; he's easy to hang with. His wife has already explained him to himself, and best of all for you, he's safe. You don't want a commitment. He's perfect for you."

I had to agree with him.

Phoenicia

I wanted to be friends with Phoenicia, so I lent her a book. It was a special book about Chekhov and his mistress, Olga, his favorite actress who later became his wife. It was a tiny book full of intimate stories and anecdotes about the two of them. I had never heard of it; neither had Phoenicia, and since we both thought Chekhov was the best of all possible playwrights, it occurred to me that he might support me in my effort at this friendship.

Phoenicia worked a great deal more often than I did and got better parts. I wanted to study her close up, to find out how she functioned and got jobs so I could improve my skills in that area.

The book didn't help at all. Every time I saw Phoenicia after lending it to her, she would look at me and I could see her eyes skimming through the files in her head. Then she'd say, "I have your *book*!"

And I'd say, "Oh, right." Yet she never mentioned anything about when she would return it, which pissed me off.

We played out this little scene for about ten years, but when I ran into her recently at a party at Austin's and she said "I have your *book*" for about the nine hundred and seventy-seventh time, something evil sprang up in me and I said, "Son of a bitch, Phoenicia, for Christ's sakes! Keep the goddamned book! Just stop talking about it!"

Quelle gaffe. The room became a still life.

Perfect little tears gathered in Phoenicia's eyes, not enough to run down her face and leave mascara tracks, but just enough to glisten in the soft light and cause a few guests to become entranced. "Oh, darling, do you have a hankie I could borrow?" she said.

When I handed her what I had, some toilet paper I had folded into tissues before I'd left my house, she said, "Oh, never mind. I'll ask . . . I'll ask Austin to help me." Austin had come up next to us.

"What's the matter, Faneesh? What's going on?" he said.

He looked at me. I felt a sudden empathy for Alice when she shrank in Wonderland.

"It's nothing," I said. "We're having a slight difference of opinion."

"Oh, Austin," said Phoenicia, "please be kind. I so need someone to be kind to me at this moment." She reached out to him and started to *kneel in front of him.*

Austin is a director. He never let her get to the floor. She leaned against him as he took her arm and said, "C'mon, Faneesh. Let me freshen your drink. You can tell me about it in the kitchen." He winked at me as he led her away.

I stood there going through pain, betrayal, abandonment, deprivation, impotence, fear, and rage, all climaxing in a wave of joy over the fact that I would be using every bit of this experience in my very next job, where I would cause a sensation.

"What's a Nice Girl Like You—?"

My grandmother Gwinkie left my cousin Leonard a thousand dollars when she died. He bought an airplane with it. On Sunday afternoons, if it wasn't raining, he would buzz our house in it, and we'd spill out onto the driveway—my family, the cook, the dog, and the upstairs maid—in a show of encouragement and mixed emotions. We waved, wagged, barked, and shouted, "Hey, Leonard! Call us when you get home!" Then he would dip his wings to us and fly off into the distance. He was a hero to me.

We went to the movies to see Amelia Earhart flying the same plane with the engine in its nose. At the end of the film, she flew solo into the sunset to save the country, as a collective shiver ran down our spines.

It was Amelia Earhart whose name I carved into the beech tree where I spent the summer reading *Black Beauty, Greyfriars Bobby,* and *Toby Tyler or Ten Weeks with a Circus.* Leonard was my godfather. I adored him. Amelia Earhart, twenty-four feet tall on the silver screen at the Claridge Theatre, was a hero. I wanted to be her.

The Lone Ranger called to me as well. Over the radio, I heard his distant "Hi-ho, Silver, away!" backed up by the William Tell Overture as he rode off into the night. His business was saving lives and towns in the Wild West, far from Montclair in time and place. I wanted to be him, too.

Gracie Allen, another hero, also beckoned. I felt lonely and different from the rest of my classmates, and she made me laugh as I lay in bed at night after a long day at school. She cheered me every time George Burns put her down and she put him on. She was a model of built-in self-esteem.

My heroes were loners like me. In my dreams, I could fly off into the distance like Amelia on wings, the Lone Ranger on a horse, or Gracie Allen on a wave of laughter. I loved laughter, the spontaneity of it, the rush of joy around my heart.

These giants' lives were filled with adventure, while I moped around in the safe deposit box on Orange Road, where children were treated like possessions in an environment of leftover Victorian notions. I did what I was told and wondered how my heroes had escaped my fate. How did they turn their dreams into deeds? How could I claim their sense of freedom? I wanted to be all of them.

And I longed to be somebody else, not the dreary Gloomy Gus I felt I had become. An actress! That's the ticket! Actresses can be all sorts of people. I could be a hero on a stage. I could hide there.

When I got to New York, I went to every acting teacher there. I learned to be a tree and a teaspoon. I learned how to plan my actions and relate to other actors on stage. I could be "in the moment" while I created a subtext. I learned to substitute here, personalize there, never forgetting the basic sense memory on which the whole structure trembled.

A sense memory can involve any of the five senses and is meant to help the actor create a reality that isn't actually there. To see, hear, taste, touch, or smell something focuses the actor by giving him something to do. It also gives a scene a sense of truth, and colors it as well. It's the opposite of indicating or pretending. For example, if you're really cold, you will express it in an original way that will inform whatever you need to do in the scene, and you'll become a star. If you want to just walk in and stamp your feet and rub your hands together, you can become a star, too. But sense memories were the thing in many classes.

The exercise involved much questioning. Do I really see it? What color is it? How heavy is it? Is it cold against my skin? Am I really smelling a rose or just pretending? This could go on for half an hour. Then the teacher would talk at length, analyze you, go off on comparisons of Eleanora Duse and Sarah Bernhardt, tell stories of his life, and pretty soon it would be time for lunch.

Acting teachers were gods. There was Lee Strasberg, a small, gray man who looked like a tailor, on West Seventy-Second Street. He headed up the Actors Studio and argued that it took twenty years to become an actor. This implied that you would attend his classes for that amount of time. The glamorous Stella Adler, who had studied with Stanislavski for six weeks in Paris, had her own studio where she offered her students the opportunity to practice their craft by playing waiters at her dinner parties. There was the jolly, generous, roly-poly Harold Clurman, who had come up through the ranks of the Group Theatre, put on a fedora, and become a Broadway director. He held a midnight master class in scene work on top of Carnegie Hall on Thursday nights. He offered this class when he needed money for a trip to Paris. It was always exciting to be in Harold's presence, especially when he ended up standing on a chair, waving his arms, his face turning a brilliant red as he waxed passionate about the theater. I ran into him at a party once and mentioned to him that the tag from the cleaners was still on his jacket. He got so flummoxed that when he responded, it came out as gibberish. How was I to know it was the Legion of Honor pin he was wearing? I was really hopeless in those days. I trust I'm more on top of things today. There was Sandy Meisner on the East Side, reigning regally at his school, where fencing and speaking were also taught. Downtown there were Herbert Berghof and Uta Hagen, working actors, in a five-flight walk-up, a loft with no frills, just nuts and bolts. They'd show us the ropes quickly through scene work so we could go out and get a job as soon as possible.

The competition to get into the Actors Studio, a pathway to stardom, was fierce. A timed five-minute audition was required. Three members sat in judgment. If you didn't pass, you could take the audition again, like a driver's test, as often as you wanted. However, there was always a long wait, and a tremendous buildup of emotional stress. I think Geraldine Page auditioned eight times. I knew one fellow who after eleven tries with no success was planning to bomb the place. I did a few projects there for which I didn't have to be a member; it would always be a part they couldn't cast out of the studio.

A fellow in my class told me that during intermission one night in a theater lobby, a young actor threw himself at the feet of another man, grabbed him around his knees, and cried, "Please, please, I beg you, Mr. Strasberg! Take me into the Studio! Please, please, I can't go through another audition."

And with that, Stella Adler swung her umbrella and started beating the young man around his head and shoulders, saying, "You fool! Stop! Stop! That's not Lee

Strasberg! That's my husband, Harold Clurman! Get away, now. Be gone!" I believe this story.

When Marlon Brando came along, the Actors Studio bloomed, and "emotional memories" and "private moments" took hold. An emotional memory is a way of exploring an important event in your life by using all five senses to recreate the place where it happened: the sights, the smells, the sounds, etc. The actor begins five minutes before the event and usually ends up in a very emotional state, crying hysterically, laughing to beat the band, and so on. Later, with practice and rehearsal, he can summon up this memory at will for a play or a scene, that demands extraordinary emotional expression.

A private moment is an activity you wouldn't be caught dead doing if anyone were watching. The fact that about thirty people in the class were looking on confused me.

These exercises are good for homework. When you get to doing a play, there's an integration within the actor and you go to the first rehearsal, as Ben Kingsley suggests, with the lines learned or not. Your choice.

I was grateful to Michael Pollard, who joined the class fresh from high school and chose to drink a glass of orange juice as his first sense memory exercise. He got on stage down center, put his hand out in front of him, curled his fingers around some air, raised it to his mouth, and drank the whole thing down in four gulps. Then he put the glass down, patted his stomach, and beamed at us. He had just done a half-hour exercise in about a minute. He was wonderful to watch, standing there glowing, pleased, naked, and knowing.

I was simultaneously appalled and thrilled by him. That was the day Marilyn Monroe called Michael and said, "Hello, Michael? This is Marilyn, from class? I was wondering if you'd do a scene with me from *Breakfast at Tiffany's*."

Soon after that, he was starring with Warren Beatty and Faye Dunaway in *Bonnie and Clyde*.

Years later, I met a director at the Moscow Art Theatre and asked him his opinion on how the Stanislavsky method of acting was taught and practiced in the States. He thought for a moment and said, "Well, we believe in moving on."

I'm a slow learner. My intuition is fabulous, yet I don't trust it because of my suspicious nature. So I need time to get it all together. I also have trouble establishing intimacy, except when I'm onstage. There I can be intimate at the drop of a hat, especially if the house is full. The exchange of energy with the audience makes me high. The speed of the learning that happens during a performance can take your breath away. Here's an example:

The House of Blue Leaves was originally staged at the O'Neill Playwrights Conference. It was presented on a wooden platform facing bleachers and had a beech tree as a backdrop. I played Bunny, the girlfriend. Topping my excited summation of the pope's visit to New York, I got to say the last line of the first act. Laughter exploded with such force that I felt it punch me in my stomach and make me gasp as the lights went down. Yet it didn't hurt. I loved it. It was a complete connection as the audience and I traded energy. I found out how to play the scene, the audience was handed a hilarious truth, and a good time was had by all. Good theater is a great teacher.

To be an actor is to experience freedom. I got to be all kinds of people and to say and do things I could never get away with in life. When I was a junior in college, I started out in a tiny stock company of college actors and played Elvira, the gorgeous ghost in *Blithe Spirit* by Noel Coward, and ended up decades later as Madame Arcati, the medium who calls Elvira back from the other side. In The Threepenny Opera, I got to enter from the bedroom scratching my crotch on my way downstage to sing "What's the Use?" I played a lesbian lusting for another woman in *The Children's Hour.* I can be the villain, the hero, and the clown and never have to answer for anything that happens while the curtain is up. Somebody else wrote the script.

My job is to take off the mask of caution I wear in life, stop holding my breath, and really *breathe.* It's not the usual fight-or-flight breath in the top of my chest and shoulders. It's a deep breath that extends down into the root of my body, where life begins and ends. Opera singers and dancers call it the crotch breath. Onstage, I breathe like this. It connects me with my body. I give up controlling with my mind and turn everything over to my subconscious, which speaks out, surprising me and everyone around me with what's really going on inside me while I pretend to be somebody else. It's called getting naked. It's the most satisfying experience I know. It's like standing on a cliff and diving into an unknown river time after time. It's freedom from fear. It's an athletic event. It's shameless. It's sexy. It's heroic.

It takes a lot of nerve to be an actor, to get up there onstage in a play that could be good or bad. You can't ever be sure, but you do it as if it's the best play ever to come down the pike. I was in a new play early in my career, and a disgruntled playwright showed up before a preview looking for the author because he wanted to kill him. He pulled a knife out to prove it. Two of the actors, heroes both, chased him out of the theater and up Seventh Avenue for a couple of blocks before turning back. They would have chased him farther, but they had a curtain waiting and it's more fun being a hero onstage than off.

I love their company.

ACT III: CALIFORNIA

"What is the stars? What is the stars?"

—Captain Boyle in Juno and the Paycock by Sean O'Casey

Vanna White

The day Vanna White won the job of turning the letters on television's *Wheel of Fortune*, she was fighting the despair of unemployment. She was facing "the dark night of the soul." She had to take her mind off her career going down the drain before it even got started. *I'll clean out the garage*, she thought. *That will cheer me up.*

So she put on some gloves, and after a few hours of sorting, lifting, throwing out, cleaning, sweeping, and sweating in the heat of a Los Angeles afternoon, the phone rang. It was her agent.

"Vanna, they want to see you over at NBC this afternoon. Can you get there by 3:10?"

"It's three thirty now, Teddy. I could never make it."

"Yes, you could. Just hop on up Laurel Canyon, and you're there."

"I'm a mess. I've been cleaning out the garage. Could I go on a call-back?"

"No. This is the day. It's now or never."

"Well, okay, but I've got to take a shower."

"That's my girl," Teddy said, and he hung up.

When Vanna put down the phone, she realized that she was in no shape to go to an audition. She'd never get the job in her current state of exhaustion. There would be hundreds of girls competing who had washed their hair just that morning, so she finished up in the garage instead.

At six o'clock, the phone rang again. It was Teddy. He was excited.

"You got it!" he said.

"I didn't go," she said.

"You didn't go?" he said.

"No, I didn't go," she said.

"But you got it!"

What happened was that at the end of the day, the casting people took all the head shots and spread them out on the floor to remind themselves of who had been there. During the day, they had each made critical notes on the back of each actress's picture. Because the back of Vanna's picture was blank, they decided there was nothing wrong with her and that they had all loved her unconditionally. And that's how she got the job on *Wheel of Fortune* and won the fame and riches she deserved.

So goes the story

Where Do You Stay out There?

I missed out on the sixties—the flower children, the Vietnam War, Bo Diddly. My life was filled with acting in plays, so there was no time for a "real life" beyond the stage. I was guest starring in regional theater that whole decade, in Boston, Philadelphia, Palm Beach, Coconut Grove, Hartford, New Haven, Williamstown, Minneapolis, Denver. I would "job in" for a particular part in a play that couldn't be cast from within the permanent company. It would be a kind of offbeat character that would have been considered outside the range of the usual leading lady type. A leading lady was like a straight man who could move around from part to part throughout the season in variations of herself. I was too much of a character actor to do that. It was a somewhat precarious way for an actress to earn her bread and butter, but it suited me. I didn't want to be out of town for a whole season. I didn't want to lose touch with New York. I never mastered the art of being the new kid on the block, but the parts were great and the plays were classics: Shakespeare, Shaw, Molière, Coward, Wycherley.

It was good training. The plays were well written, the characters were bigger than life, and the words were the literature of drama. In order to perform in these plays, I had to stretch every fiber of my body and brain to fulfill the roles. They demanded big emotions and bold comedy, and if you could master them and remain believable, you were in good shape.

I didn't want to spend the rest of my life being a gypsy, packing suitcases and collecting unemployment insurance. I had a five-year plan for when the next lull came: California. TV and Film. Then everyone would know me, and I'd get to act on the stage in New York all the time. That will be the fulfillment of my dream. I got out the I Ching sticks, and they said, "Go to California." So I went.

When I first got there, I stayed with Frances, my best friend from New York, and I found that I could no longer talk to her. She was deeply involved in Werner Erhard's self-improvement program, EST, which scared me because it had changed her personality from when I knew her back east. EST was a form of mind control consisting of meditation and brainwashing techniques. Large groups of people paid lots of money to sit in hotel ballrooms for three days while "trainers" insulted and berated them, telling them to "be in the present" and "get it." This would be followed by periods of relaxation during which they would sometimes lie on the floor and listen to a visualization conducted by the trainer. It was a post—New Age cult that practiced mind over matter with the goal of success dancing in your near future.

Frances had become a stranger. She seemed to be on a different page than I was, with things going on in her head that I wasn't let in on. Her horizons extended way beyond mine. She was on a stairway to the stars. I was simply after the next job.

She lived with her husband in one of the mansions lining the wide, leafy streets of Beverly Hills. The first thing she said to me after "hello" and a hug was, "I want you to see my orchard." We went through the back door, and she pointed to some frail saplings spaced in a haphazard manner right in front of us. She moved through them like a kind of wood nymph and spoke as if in a dream.

"This is a cherry tree . . . and that's an apple tree . . . a grapefruit tree. This one's an orange tree." She patted it. "A lemon and a lime . . . a fig tree." She gazed off somewhat vaguely and said, "Over there is jasmine and a grapevine and some mint. This is my orchard. Doesn't it smell great? I'm working on bottling it and selling it as a perfume to Neiman Marcus. They want to call it Redondanse. It's got a nice resonance to it, don'cha think? I buy all my clothes there now. And there's my Olympic-size swimming pool. I don't swim in it anymore. I was swimming in it every day, but my hair started falling out. So I stopped."

"Oh, Frances, I'm so sorry," I said.

"That's all right. It'll grow back. Do you like the wig?"

"Oh, I didn't realize—well, yes."

Then she showed me her scream room. We had both been in scream therapy in New York. We had sat in a group therapy circle and screamed at one another while a shrink monitored us with comments like, "Go ahead, Peggy. Get it out," and "Louder, louder. Let us hear you."

Then he'd put Frances in a celebrity group because she'd made a wonderful movie. I had a small part in the movie as a member of a therapy group, but the only time I was in the celebrity group with Frances in real life was when the secretary made a mistake and put me there by accident. I was extremely uncomfortable. The group was filled with celebrities and their wives or husbands, and I was sitting there, a nobody, doing my best to scream with the rest of them, when suddenly I went unconscious. When I came to, Frances was sobbing and the doctor was saying, "Peggy, why do you hate, hate, hate Frances and wish she were dead?"

I was in a daze and didn't know what he was talking about. Everybody in the room was uncomfortable. Then the doctor told Frances and me to hug each other, which seemed to me somewhat unproductive. We did as he told us, but it was never the same between us again, although we pretended it was.

Now here she was showing me her scream room in the den in California. It contained a soundproof padded area under a bed so as not to disturb the neighbors, who had complained. The cook, the chauffeur, the maid, and the secretary were urged to use it as well.

There was a full-length portrait of Frances in the living room from the set of one of her movies, and it dominated the large, high-ceilinged, many-windowed space to such an extent that when Frances was in there as well, I couldn't think straight.

She spent a lot of time staring at me, and I would start to giggle. She would say, "What are you laughing at?"

"I don't know," I would tell her. "You're staring at me, and I don't know what to say."

So I had to move. We had been close friends for ten years, seeing each other or talking on the phone every day. And now we had nothing in common, not even my boyfriends, to whom she had often taken a fancy in the past. What we'd had in common was our hunger to act and work, and now there was this huge gap between us. I didn't measure up in this strange, foreign setting; I didn't even want to.

I wanted to act, and she wanted to be a star with all the fringe benefits: the best table at the restaurant, the VIP upgrade on the airplane, celebrity parties, awards, limousines, clothes, hairdressers, trainers, stuff I didn't even know about. I had an orange Rent-a-Wreck car parked in her driveway, and, like me, it just didn't fit in at Frances's place. I will always remember her generosity, but it cost too much.

A Gypsy

I took to the hills. I sublet a house from an actress named Jennifer who was trying to live on both coasts at once. After I moved in, she called and asked if she could come and stay with me.

"I'll sleep in the attic," she said. "You won't even know I'm there."

So back she came with her dachshund, whose name was Tom. We chatted for a while. Jennifer talked at great length about her lovers, and then she pulled a ladder of stairs down from the hall ceiling and said a cheery good night. Tom tried to climb up after her but couldn't make it as his legs were too short and his belly sagged and scraped the risers. He had to stay downstairs with me. He was infuriated by this and went around peeing on all the furniture.

In the morning, I told Jennifer that I didn't think it was right what was happening. I had just had all the furniture covers cleaned, and now they were going to smell bad again. She seemed shocked and hurt.

"Heavens, I never dreamed I would be made to feel *persona non grata* in my own home!" she said.

"Well, that's the way I feel," I said and went into the kitchen to do the dishes she'd left in the sink because I didn't want the ants trailing in.

After some marathon phoning, she took off, leaving me a check for $3.21. I assumed it was her estimate for sub-subletting the attic for a night.

That year in that house, I turned fifty—old no matter how you looked at it, and older than that if you lived in Hollywood. It was even older if you lived alone in a house where a dog had peed on the furniture. *There was an old woman who lived in a shoe.* I called my sister in tears. What was to become of me, a fifty-year-old gypsy?

"Oh, Peggy. After fifty everything gets so much better," said Adeline. She sounded so sure of it that I believed her. She wasn't acting in order to cheer me up. I was the actress. She was the writer. I could tell the difference.

Starting over

Finding work in LA was like looking for an oasis in a desert. It was another medium in another country. When I first got there, it was Halloween. I went to the bank to open an account. It was only ten in the morning, and the tellers were all dressed up to go trick-or-treating. I had a choice of Clark Gable, a skeleton, or the Wicked Witch from *The Wizard of Oz*. I picked Clark Gable and asked him if he'd give me some play money as I was going to be working in films now. He didn't get it. He said he was writing a script.

LA was the first time I saw bank tellers in costume on Halloween.

In LA, thinking I should review my acquaintance with the local movie culture and re-read *What Makes Sammy Run?* By Budd Schulberg I got a blank look from the salesgirl in the book store and after she thought it through she said, "Maybe try the children's section in the back." Wctch up on the c

My first job in Hollywood was a part in *Oh, God!* starring George Burns. I had met the director, Carl Reiner, when he was casting offbeat types for the opening scene, in a supermarket. There were no lines. It was an establishing shot, from which the audience gets the style and place and tone of what's to come. It was also background for the titles, and for the latecomers who were still getting seated and generally annoying the rest of the moviegoers.

Carl was one of my heroes. I had adored him since I'd heard him interview Mel Brooks as the 2000 Year Old Man. When I got to the set, Carl looked at me as if he'd forgotten who I was. Then he said, "Oh, oh, I know. Go over there and shoplift a lamb chop. Put it under your raincoat. Wardrobe, get her a raincoat!" I saw the film recently and thought I was fabulous, a natural, experienced, desirable and on my way. But I don't think anyone else ever noticed me. It may always be Carl's and my secret.

Then there was a long period of going on interviews. I was a new kid on the block, and a call for a reading meant that I had to go in and read three different times for three different episodes of the same show over the course of several weeks before the casting people felt they knew me well enough. Then they'd take a chance and have me in for the director.

Thinking I wasn't going to get a job for a while, I tried out for a part in a play at a little theater at the east end of Santa Monica Boulevard. LA stage work at that time left something to be desired. Actors might leave a production at any moment if they were offered a TV show or a film. Someone else was always ready to go on as a replacement at the last minute. The play would suffer, but what the hell. Actors were out there to break into movies and television, where the money was. Acting on stage in LA served mainly to keep one's chops salivating. Actors ran the risk of rehearsing alone with just the director while the other actors in the scene were off auditioning for screen roles.

Then I got a call to read for *Barney Miller.* I went, not expecting to get it, and didn't think to mention the play I was in, *Midnight Moon at the Greasy Spoon,* as I didn't think they'd be interested. When I got the call to be on *Barney Miller,* I found that it would involve working during the week the play began performances. I'd have to miss opening night.

Steeped in theater tradition as I was, I didn't think about it. I couldn't leave the play in the lurch like that. The theater is a temple. You just don't do that.

My agent was bewildered.

"But, Peggy, we've got to get you started," she said.

I was firm and went to rehearsal at the theater. The first preview was to be the next day. When I got there, I learned that they hadn't gotten me a costume yet. Fate was taking care of me. I thought of the I Ching sticks that had told me to come here. I had turned down *Barney Miller,* one of the foremost TV shows of the time, for a stage play in East LA where they had no clothes for me to wear. I started to have second and third and fifth thoughts. It got to be midnight and then one o'clock. At two o'clock in the morning, I said to my room at the Sunset Marquis, "I gotta talk to someone about this."

There was an old character actor in the compound whose light was always on. I knocked on his door.

"Come in," he said.

I told him my story.

"Emory," I said, "do you think I made a mistake?"

"Ye-e-e-s," he drawled, deadpan. "I think you did."

At nine o'clock the next morning, I called Marsha, my agent, and asked her if I could change my mind, if she thought they had cast it yet.

She said she'd find out.

I was very lucky. They still wanted me. I went to meet Danny Arnold, the producer/writer/director. When I got out of the elevator, the casting director was there to meet me. She was as white as a sheet washed in too much Clorox. I'd never seen anyone so white before.

"Are you all right?" I asked.

"I didn't get much sleep last night," she said. "C'mon, let's go."

She pushed me back into the elevator, and we were off to another floor. I found out later that she had almost lost her job because of me. No one turned down *Barney Miller.* Everyone in town would kill to be on it. She'd had a huge scare. I felt awful about causing her such a fright and relieved that she went on to bigger and better jobs.

Danny Arnold was an actor's guardian angel. Before he wrote a guest part, he would cast the actor so the two would fit together like a hand in glove. And they were outrageous parts. I played a cat burglar's widow who was carrying on her husband's business. Still very much in love with him, I was cat burglaring because it made me feel close to him. After that, I played a woman who made a date through a personals ad, and, when the guy arrived and pulled out a gun to rob her, she shamed him into first eating the dinner she'd cooked for him. Another time, I took the police station hostage with a pressure cooker that I said had a bomb in it, because I thought the police were responsible for my husband's impotence. I also played a woman who became so engrossed in soap operas that she thought she was seeing real life through a window in her apartment. She would call the station and report crimes and clues from the plots. These women weren't me, yet they were because Danny wrote them for me. He slanted and filtered them through me, as he slanted and filtered all of the characters on the show through the actors.

The regular cast was based on aspects of Danny's own personality; he split himself up into five guys. It worked well. The stories were true, taken from actual New York City police files, and the set was a copy of the Sixty-Eighth Street precinct.

It was the first time I heard actors talking no louder than a whisper to each other. It was quiet as a laboratory on that set. It was my introduction to "less is more" on camera. Keep your head still and do nothing. It's all in the eyes. Danny would stand close by and act silently with the actor.

He also laughed so quietly that the mike couldn't pick it up, but the actor could. This gave us a "live" audience—a gift that makes for a better performance. If you don't believe this, try telling yourself a joke in an empty hall and see how funny it isn't.

Danny used four cameras shooting simultaneously from different angles, cutting down on the number of takes and keeping the spontaneity of the scene. It normally takes five days to film a half hour sitcom, but Barney Miller was so well written that one year we did a complete show on the last day of shooting before the season's contract was up. At midnight, they would have to dip into "golden time" and pay triple the salaries. Hal Linden and I did a six-minute scene—walking, talking, opening file cabinets, drinking coffee, getting up, sitting down, taking out a gun, and strapping it on—in one take.

In the episode where I watched the soaps, I got to say, "Only his chauffeur knows for sure" about a corrupt judge. It was a take-off on a catchphrase of the day about a blonde and her hairdresser. I'm quite certain that scene helped Noam Pitlik, the director, win an Emmy.

Hal Linden and his regular staff of officers, Steve Landesberg, Ron Glass, Max Gail, Ron Carey and Jack Soo were amazing actors and lovable, real people and always applauded the guest actors when their work was finished. It was the first time I'd experienced that.

Danny Arnold was a tremendous talent with the energy to work around the clock on a production. He made everybody look good. I was lucky to have been there to look good, too.

Billy Crystal

Billy Crystal was the coolest of them all. When I was on *Soap* a fellow actor asked him how he prepared for the late-night talk shows he'd been doing, and he said he "mulled" about it. He said it was simple: Go into your subconscious and just mull it over. Then say whatever comes out. Of course, he started very young, growing up surrounded by musicians and the unconditional love and support of his family. He was a veteran by the time he got to *Soap*.

The first time I appeared as a guest on the show, it was the second year for this huge hit. The ratings were solid, and it had a long run ahead of it. I was used to planning everything and rehearsing over and over, so I was horrified to find that in rehearsing with this cast, whenever there was a break for the cameramen to mark their positions, the actors immediately started talking about real estate or swimming pools or vacations in Bali.

We had just run through the scene for the first time and were on a break while the set was being lit. The cast was standing around talking about houses and finding the right one, the right neighborhood, the right price. Blah-de-blah, blah-blah.

I tried to keep quiet, but I couldn't manage it. I broke into the conversation with, "Why don't we rehearse the scene? It could use some work, don'cha think?"

There was a long, deadly silence, and then Billy Crystal stepped in and saved me. He said, like it was a new concept, "Oh, yeah. That's a good idea. Let's try that. Let's go over it again and see if we can make it better."

Everybody joined in to make me feel at ease, and it wasn't until long afterward that I realized that actors in sitcoms keep fresh by not rehearsing too much. It would be like analyzing a comic strip; it would die on you. The trick is to stay in the present and not pretend that what you're doing is great literature. Let the writer do that. Just say the lines. You were cast for your quality when you walked in the door. It's a first-impression kind of thing, so please don't rock the boat. Mull instead. What a concept.

The Importance of Being Seen

On New Year's Day at the beach in Santa Monica at the end of Sunset Boulevard, the Penguins meet at noon and swim around a Coast Guard lifeboat in the ocean to celebrate the event. The water in California at that time is usually no colder than about 56 degrees, but the TV news stations cover the event anyway. It's of great interest, mainly to the Penguins, who go for pancakes afterward and then rush home to see themselves on the six o'clock news.

It's fascinating to me that part of this group is made up of actors who are already on TV and in films, and still they gather around the set at six and scream:

"Oh, there we are!"

"There I am!"

"Oh, there's Dickie!"

"Where?"

"Where?"

" . . . and Patty."

"I don't see them. Say, what's that old guy doing in there?"

"Dunno."

Actors are always devising ways to be seen because they're constantly looking for the next job. In LA, it's tricky. There are plenty of parties and tennis games and restaurants, yet half of an actor's life is spent trying to get to them in the isolation of gridlock and road rage.

One year, a Penguin friend of mine missed New Year's in the ocean because he got stuck in bumper-to-bumper traffic on the freeway. The fellow in the car behind him kept bumping him and blowing his horn, and then he cut in front of him and sped down an off ramp. The Penguin got so mad that he followed his tormentor home to find out where he lived. This caused the Penguin to miss being at the beach and on the news, so he went home and sulked. Then, in the dead of night, he went back to squeeze epoxy glue into the keyholes of the offender's car. It was a social life for which I was growing too old.

I had another friend, Tom, who got arrested for singing while driving on the freeway. Traffic was moving so slowly that he'd sung all the songs he knew and had started referring to some sheet music on the seat beside him. It looked to a highway patrolman as if Tom were reading while he drove. The judge asked Tom to sing a song for him. When Tom finished singing, the judge said that he couldn't possibly punish someone for loving music as much as Tom obviously did. He wished him luck and let him go.

Rain in California mixes with the oil from the cars on the roads, which become as slippery as ice and cause many cars to skid into one another. Tempers grow as foul as the weather. Drivers blow horns at red lights and mix it up while angled toward each other along the streets. Lawyers, insurance companies, and drivers divide the money three ways.

When I needed to refresh my soul because of this madness, I would meet Angela Crockett, an actress friend, at the LA County Museum for a healthy salad and a couple or three pastries—we would split the third, as we were both on diets—and we would vent.

I always parked behind the museum so I could walk past the tar pits there. A fake dinosaur screamed silently as she appeared to sink into the black ooze. A panther still chewing on a mouthful of flesh from his last victim was about to be sucked under the same way. The scene always reminded me of a Disney cartoon gone wrong.

I was trying to break into voice-over work at the time. It paid well—into the six figures, I was told. The field, of course, was dominated by men who had been cutups and class clowns since third grade. I knew one of them, Jackson, who liked nothing better than to call up Severn Darden, an original 2nd City Improv actor from the Days of Mike Nichols and Elaine May. You couldn't get any better. So Jackson would call up Severn and talk to him in Severn's voice. It would drive Severn crazy because he would have to talk to himself and not know who he was.

There were about three women who could do forty voices apiece, including mine, so the competition was fierce. But you never know what can happen unless you try. In California, you had to live from fluke to fluke. One lucky break, and you'd be in. I'd done everything else, so I figured this might be possible too, and I didn't have to look young or dress up and wear makeup to the auditions, which was becoming an issue for me in my formidable forties.

I found Angela with the Dutch Masters. She was packed into a black fitted suit with a ruffled, cream-colored collar and cuffs and black T-strap shoes. A squashy black tam was settled loosely atop her faded curls. She seemed to belong more to the forties, wandering through the Metropolitan with Alice and the Mad Hatter hovering in the background, than to the eighties among the tar pits of La Brea.

We eavesdropped on a docent cultivating her voice as she discussed the paintings with a cluster of eight-year-olds. Some of the children were looking at ships about to be caught in a storm. Sailors struggled to reef the sails and save their lives and cargo. One child had started to cry, some were becoming restless, and the others had sat down on the floor in a politely rebellious manner. The docent, her agenda intact, proceeded, "Now what do you think Holland would put in all those boats to send throughout the world in such a storm?"

"Cocoa!" Angela sang out, startling the children and causing the crying child to scream. Angela had performed the classics in large theaters.

"Oh, that takes me back," she turned to me. "We drank cocoa in the WAVES. Let's go get some." She had served as a lieutenant in the Women's Auxiliary of the U.S. Navy during World War II, which she said had been the happiest time of her life.

Leaving the chaos she had caused behind us, we fled to the cafeteria, where coffee won out over cocoa because of the calories. We ripped into a couple of salads, which turned out, we agreed, to be pretty good for museum food, especially with the roasted peppers instead of loose California raisins.

"Those raisins make a salad look like a rabbit strolled through it," I said.

"I have to call Thayer," said Angela. "Check in, see if his agent called, if he needs a ride. You know he's terrified of driving. Since they took away his license, I drive him everywhere—appointments, work, rehearsals, basketball, everywhere."

I wondered if she was still annoyed with me for having sung "Windflowers" at their anniversary party. She *had* said, "Just bring something that doesn't cost anything—a poem or a song or something you've baked." But my half-baked rendition of "Windflowers" from *The Golden Apple* had seemed to cast a pall over the party. It's a song about Penelope waiting for Ulysses to come home from the wars. She's fearful of growing old during the passing years, yet it turns into a testament to her love for him, which will keep them both young forever. It's a gorgeous song, but in Hollywood, the mention of growing old is simply in very poor taste, and once again I had felt out of the loop.

Angela, mouth full or empty, talked nonstop. She spoke all of her subtext all of the time. It was the kind of chatter that I strove not to hear in myself or others, the ever-repetitive tapes. Yet Angela could hear, free-associate, and incorporate what was said to her and steam on like a UN interpreter. I admired her facility even as it got on my nerves. *Why can't she just talk to me one-on-one?* In the middle of my tomato, I started to cry.

"I'm sorry. I can't help it. It has nothing to do with you," I lied.

Angela immediately assimilated me into her stream of consciousness.

"I noticed the tears in your eyes. Could you pass the guava? I have a little bit of bread left."

"I don't want to make you feel bad," I said.

"Darling, you're the one who feels bad. What is it? Is there something I can do?"

She reached across the table to comfort me, brushing her sleeve through the salad on the way.

"No," I said.

I handed her a napkin so she could wipe the dressing off her cuff and said, "I don't know what it's coming from. Mostly it happens when I look, really look, into someone's eyes. They don't look back anymore. They don't see me. They look right through me. Do you know what I mean? I feel isolated. I feel invisible."

The hot flashes and sweating that were now happening every time I ate were coming on. I jabbed at a carrot. It slid across the table onto the floor.

"I saw that," said Angela in an attempt to lighten things up.

I plowed on. "It can be anyone," I said. "Man, woman, child—well, no, not so much children—animals, especially dogs, not so much cats. There's always this possibility of looking into someone's soul and actually getting in there, inside of someone—and more, letting them climb inside of me . . ."

Angela's response was, "I wonder if we should keep sitting here. Look at, uh . . ., there's all those, uh, people . . . standing."

"We're having coffee. Let's get another cup," I said, my misery shifting into truculence.

"I'll get it," she said. "Oh, I wonder, do they give you another cup? Do they give you a second cup free? Where should I go? What? What should I, ah . . . ?"

She couldn't decide whether to get up or sit down.

"You get it, Angela. I'll hold the table. Here's some money."

"No, no, no. It's free. It's probably free. What do you think? It's probably free. What?"

"Well, go see. Here's fifty cents just in case."

Angela was off.

I reached over and picked the linen napkin out of her salad. I felt less alone then than when she had been sitting with me. I sat back and thought about Jessie. I often ran into Jessie at casting calls. At the café across from Paramount, drinking wine in a dark booth after an audition, Jessie had told me that she had been horribly depressed herself, beyond anything I could imagine. That's why she'd gotten a face-lift.

Then she started bragging about her husband, a surgeon who drilled sinuses and did extremely creative work. How was drilling sinuses creative? I wondered if she'd ever seen *Kings Row*, where Ronald Reagan wakes up from an operation and finds his legs missing and says, "Where's the rest of me?" I should have told her about Dad's friend who left the scissors behind when he took out an appendix, charged his patient for a second operation to remove the scissors, and then went off to Europe for a vacation.

Competition for recognition—I was sick of it. I didn't care if I never did another commercial. In New York, in the last one I was up for—it was for Dove soap—the sponsor asked me if I could just give them an idea of how I might fly around the room. I said, "No," and left. Apparently Georgia Engel was able to do it. Well, at least I don't have a lisp.

"Here, I got it!" Angela was back, waving coffee cups.

I put my napkin in the saucer under my cup.

"Have you seen Jessie recently?" I said.

"Oh, that Jessie. She can really fertilize a problem," said Angela.

"Yes. Do you know what she told me? She got angry at me for something or other and said, 'You know, you can really dish it out, but you can't take it!' So I went over to her the next time I saw her to straighten it out. She was in her car, and she said, 'I don't want to be friends with you anymore. You don't understand.' In one hundred-and-one-degree heat, she rolled up her window and started changing her blouse."

"Oh, she's toxic," said Angela. "What were you, at an audition?"

"Yeah."

"I never change clothes between auditions."

"How old do you think she is?" I said.

"Fifties. Fifty. She's gotta be fifty if she's a day. I would say fifty. I heard she went somewhere, I think Romania, for the summer for those youth treatments."

"You can get that stuff here," I said. "It doesn't work. I took a bottle of it to the pharmacy at Cedars-Sinai to have it analyzed. The pharmacist told me to hold the bottle in my right hand next to my heart and to hold my other hand stretched out in front of me. Then he took hold of that wrist and pushed my arm down twice. It kept rising of its own accord, so he said not to take any. It wouldn't agree with me."

"Really? A holistic pharmacist?" said Angela. "At Cedars-Sinai?"

"Yes. They have an art gallery there too."

"I didn't know that."

"In the halls on the celebrity floor, for the patients to look at while they're recovering."

Angela finished her coffee, then emptied the cream pitcher into her cup and drank it down.

"I'd like to go to that sleeping spa in Switzerland," I said.

"What's that? I never heard of it."

"You sleep for a month while they feed you intravenously, inject lamb fetuses into your veins, and wake you up twenty years younger. Like Rip Van Winkle in reverse. Ann Miller does it every other year."

"I love my Doctor Cary. He did my eyes and my neck, you know." Angela made a fleeting swipe at her tam, which flopped around on her head as if it were alive before settling back on her overflowing curls.

"I know. You told me. How long were you black-and-blue?"

"Oh, a couple of minutes, that's all. You know something interesting? This is why I love him so much, Cary. He told me that if you're happy and content when you do it, you don't get black-and-blue."

"I've been very conflicted," I said. "I've done a lot of research, and I have come to the conclusion that I want to look real. I want to look like who I am. 'My face, I don't mind it because I'm behind it. It's the ones in the front get the jar. (a long ago quote from my father.) So the hell with it. No way, and that's that. Finished. Over and out . . . . Why are you looking at me like that?"

"Well, you could just do the . . . a little . . . just a little here," Angela patted under her chin with the back of her hand to demonstrate. "And here, the eyes. That's just fatty tissue. That's nothing. He takes pictures first. And he blows them up, oh, poster-size. That's what the operates from."

"I know, like you're not even there while he's operating!" I said. "I went for a consultation once. I just wanted that, what you got—just the eyes. He did his own photography. He told me to grasp my eyelids in the middle, squint, pull them out, and let go. The lids stayed out there reaching into the room about fifty feet, frozen in three-dimensional folds, *trompe l'oeil* effect for the poster. Then he clicked away and said he wanted to do all kinds of other things, too, like move my scalp around because my brow had fallen. I hadn't even known my brow had fallen!"

"Oh, go to my guy. You'll love him."

"I can't bear the idea of black-and-blue. I think I would get very black-and-blue. Maybe I'll go over Christmas—kill two birds with one stone."

"If you could get in," Angela said. She took a compact out of her purse, powdered her nose, then positioned the mirror slightly to her left and said, "Look at that old lady tottering around behind me. She looks like she's on her last legs, going to fall over any minute. Maybe we'd better . . . oh, she got a table."

Art lovers were eyeing us unpleasantly.

"Here's what I truly, deep down, feel, I think," I said, dragging Angela back to the subject. "Beautiful women get face-lifts so they can stay beautiful. Character women don't need them."

"Well, you don't need one."

I looked at Angela to see in what she had meant by that remark, but she was scavenging in her purse for loose change.

"It's important to get old and look cheerful, not tired," I said. "If you're old and tired-looking, people get nervous and, of course, they're not going to see you."

"Oh, I absolutely agree with you," said Angela. "The best person to be around is a jolly old one." Now she was searching the floor for a coin she had dropped.

I thought of Munch and *The Scream*. My ears were ringing, and silver zigzag circles from too much coffee danced in front of my eyes. At any minute, I was going to go blind.

"Can I have your autograph?" The waitress offered a pen and a paper napkin for me to sign.

"Sure." I read her name tag, wrote "Best wishes to Jo Anne," and signed it, leaving a small blot for an *e* on the porous napkin so that my name looked like *Peggy Pop*.

"Thanks. I really like your work," she said. "I can't remember what I've seen you in, but I recognize your face."

"Oh, good. Thanks for asking."

"That's okay. I hope you don't mind, but we really need your table, and you've been sitting here forever."

"Sure. We were just going," I said.

"I have to call Thayer again," said Angela.

"I know."

"See if he needs a ride," we said together.

Angela disappeared into the crowd.

That's what I was going to do, disappear like the dinosaur I had to walk by to get to my car. That dinosaur had a lot more wrinkles than I did. I wanted to reach over, pat her, and tell her that wrinkles were fine. Stop worrying. But of course she wouldn't be able to hear me. She was busy sinking into a tar pit.

I looked at the sky. A storm was coming. My watch said quarter of four. If I didn't dawdle, I could beat the road rage home.

Acting with Olivier

LA. Mid-eighties. A baby backyard behind a small Hollywood bungalow off of Melrose. Ten a.m.

I was watering crabgrass, so hot from the sun that it burned my bare feet. Half the water evaporated before it hit the ground, and the rest sent up steam when it landed. I thought of my father paying me fifty cents a basket to remove crabgrass from our lawn in Montclair. Breathing was torture as the air burned the inside of my nose with every breath. To quench my thirst, I picked a honeysuckle blossom, only to find that its nectar had turned sour. The old man next door was peering over the fence, doing his ten a.m. ogling. It was desperately quiet except for the birds fighting in my fig tree and the occasional plane flying back to New York.

I cursed the pain as sweat dribbled into my eyes, left some salt, and trickled on down my neck. "I'm an actress, for Christ's sake!" I yelled. The birds left immediately. The old man laughed.

I summed up my life for myself. I was chained to a mortgage because Frank, my real estate friend, had told me, "Otherwise the government gets all your money." What money?

I'll take the taxes. I didn't have a job, would probably never work again, was in California acting hell, and had an old man laughing at me!

The phone rang. I reached through the barred window and seized it. It was my agent with the brush cut.

"Do you want to go over to Fox for a part in *The Jazz Singer*?"

"Sure."

"It's only one line, but it's a scene with Laurence Olivier. You'd be playing his nanny."

"His what?"

"His nanny. They'll see you and Angela Crockett. Shoots this morning."

To act with Olivier—oh, my God. He might give me a tip that would change my acting life. What the hell—my *life*. For once, I was in the right place at the right time, watering my lawn. What luck.

Angela. I could get there before she could. She was probably out driving Thayer somewhere and getting lost. She didn't have a chance. I didn't even comb my hair. I could do that and put my makeup on in the car. When I drove past Angela's apartment, I saw her car parked outside. She'd be late. She later told me she was throwing up at that moment from the excitement.

The assistant director was waiting for me at Soundstage 22. He handed me a script and told me to look it over as he bustled me inside. A small man lounging in a director's chair, wearing a tennis pullover and double-thick, dark-rimmed glasses, spoke to me.

"Go ahead. Let's hear it," he said.

I took a good breath and read: "You can't go in there. He's sleeping."

"Fabulous," said the director.

"Wait—ah, wait a minute," I said. "We're not in the, uh, same room, and he's asleep. I thought we were going to be in a scene together . . . Lord Olivier and, uh . . .

I . . ."

"Oh, honey, don't worry your pretty little head. We're gonna improvise this scene."

His glasses reflected the light so I couldn't see his eyes.

"Listen," he said, "we had a fellow in here last week—just brought him in for a bit, no lines, nothing. He improvised. He was here six days. Turned into a terrific cameo. D'ya improvise?"

"Uh, yes.

"Marvelous. Take her to wardrobe, and we'll get started. Have you had lunch? Get her some lunch, Fred. We'll call you as soon as we're set up."

As we went to wardrobe, I saw Angela heading toward us. I stifled the impulse to hide.

"Hi, Angela."

"Oh, hi, Peggy. I'd stop to chat——" She almost tripped on a cable, caught herself, and laughed. "I'm on my way to an interview." She took off in a flurry of red hair and curves.

"Good luck!" I called as she waved.

Because the nanny's outfit was too small and there was no time to let it out, I had a salad for lunch. Then I got made up by a man called Shotgun who tried to sell me a tube of makeup base he'd invented, which he claimed doubled as an excellent toothpaste. His hands shook, and he said I should do my eyes myself. I thanked him and went to my dressing room, where I unbuttoned the waist of my uniform, lay down, and fell asleep from the stress.

Fred knocked on the door, saying, "Here are the rewrites, honey." He handed me an entire script and was gone. I leafed through it, looking for additional scenes with the nanny, but there were none. I skipped back to page ninety-four, where my line had been before lunch. There was no sign of it. I went looking for Fred on the soundstage, and——oh, my God——there was Olivier in a yarmulke and bedroom slippers. He walked past me, maybe eighteen inches away, and nodded. I beamed back at him and almost started to curtsy. No words were exchanged. Then he started talking to the director. I eavesdropped and heard the thrilling English accent.

"——about the fellow playing my brother."

"Yes, sir," said the director.

"He's very good, you know, but you see, he's doing a——" Sir Lawrence sucked in his breath before he went on as if to accomplish an extremely delicate task, hoping to convey that it was not his habit to tread on another director's territory. "He's doing a very subtle Jewish accent. And, ah, we have that scene together, you see, where I'm dying . . . on the bed, don't you know, and talking to him with my, ah, music hall, so to speak . . . the way *I* do, and we're in the same family, you see, and well, *I'm* going to sound like . . . ah, what can I say? Sort of, ah . . . sort of, ah . . . sort of . . . *a ham*! Do you know what I mean?"

"I'll take care of it, Sir Laurence. You needn't worry about that."

"Oh, thanks so much, old chap. Hmm. Well, it's on to four o'clock. So I think I'll be going home, eh?"

"Fine, fine. See you tomorrow."

"Righto."

Olivier headed back past me, didn't nod and was gone. I went back to my dressing room and looked in the mirror. I was still there.

Fred pounded on the door. "Get touched up and come quick as you can to the set. They're waiting for you!"

My heart clutched, my breath stumbled and my head fought the dizziness. He had scared the shit out of me.

Shotgun had disappeared. I grabbed a powder puff and patted.

When I got to the set, a small hallway on a platform at the top of some stairs with no railing, I found actors, cameramen, and crew crowded together, rehearsing the scene. I stood here and there, unable to find the director I had read for that morning. People were acting all around me. I was in the way. I got trapped in a corner and couldn't get out. The director's voice over a loudspeaker cut into the confusion.

"There are people on the set who don't belong there," he said. "I wish they would leave."

Everyone stopped. An extra coughed. A small path opened up for me. My ill-fitting white shoes from wardrobe squeaked on the floor as I slunk out.

In the dressing room, I took off my nanny costume. The assistant director apologized to me. He promised I'd get paid. I reassured him that he was a good person. I got in my car and drove home to finish watering the lawn, a task that one actually never can finish because LA is a desert.

But What Did You Do out There?

I missed New York. I had to stop reading *The New York Times* because of my longing and need to be back there, hustling and bustling with the rest of them. The running around of it, bumping into friends on the street, getting the news, the mass of culture, the worlds in the Met, the music ringing out of Lincoln Center, the seasons—blasting me in the winter, caressing and arousing me in the spring, beating me up in the summer, urging me on in the fall.

In LA the sun doesn't shine; it glares until night comes, a clap of blackness, bypassing twilight, giving no warning. It's a city built on sand, the entertainment capital that was to be the envy of the world, yet the weather—the freak storms, fires, floods, and mudslides—cannot be tamed, and the people rebuilding in their wake every year on the same sites cannot change.

Between jobs, I battled my restlessness and the flaws in my character. I learned to play an inner game of tennis. To do this, you have to get rid of your inner critic and live completely in the moment. I actually accomplished this once, and it was an extraordinary experience. I returned every ball with beautiful form, seeing each one as it approached, breathing in as I drew back my racket, breathing out as I swung, never taking my eyes off the ball, staying connected to it as if I were riding on it for the whole trip until it was returned to me, united with it until my opponent missed. I had a sense of satisfaction, completeness, and even joy at this. My teacher Zach asked me, "How did you do that?"

I threw my racquet in the air and yelled across the net to him, "I got rid of my critic! I got rid of my critic!"

"Tell me how!" he said, to reinforce the progress.

"I told him to wait in the car."

Zach almost fell over laughing. His feet kicked up in the air and he clicked his heels in front of him. My critic was a man, and he hadn't left at all.

I tried to even up my personality with a more sensitive approach. From a book, I learned to draw using the right side of my brain. First, I copied a picture that was upside down before looking at it right side up. The process made me nauseated and irritated. When I turned my picture around, I was amazed to find that I had drawn a really good copy of a man, full figure, sitting in a chair. The drawing was quite complicated; had I tried to copy him right side up, all my opinions and preconceptions about what I was seeing would have ended in chaos spilling off the page. However, not knowing what I was looking at, because it was upside down and unrecognizable, made me really "see" for the first time like an artist. It was thrilling. Then I drew a picture of a very wrinkled paper bag and was so impressed with it that I put it on the refrigerator as if I were a parent. My friends started referring to it in passing as Peggy's paper bag.

I got interested in photography and took a lot of pictures, which gave me the opportunity to look closely at people, to study them without appearing impolite, playing little scenes with them to make them be spontaneous. Afterward, I realized that the pictures I took were really always of me. They didn't look like me, but they were united by a certain style that I felt was mine: focused, real, relaxed, thinking about something specific, and, consequently, intriguing.

I spent Saturday mornings at the master class of the current acting guru and watched people take their clothes off in thoughtful, private-moment exercises. On Sundays, I went to the beach.

A salesman came down from San Francisco to hold seminars on how to channel information from the universe. He had combined sales promotion techniques with EST and Silva Mind Control. The first seminar was held in Beverly Hills and had attracted four hundred people. Early on, he went into a trance and spoke to various people in the room. He said "Don't worry so much, Peggy." I was flabbergasted. I thought, *This guy's got my number, all right.* I looked around to see if everyone was staring at me before I realized that, out of four hundred people, there were bound to be a few named Peggy. I thought, *Who the heck doesn't worry?*

The salesman had a staff of older ladies in wigs who sold four-thousand-dollar crystal earrings at the break. People were buying them. They were supposed to make the owner more attractive to the spirits. When I asked one of the staff members why they all wore wigs, she said, "We work such hard, long days and all, we don't have time to do our hair."

At dinner, we went Dutch, and the richest woman at the table ordered the fifty-six dollar salad. Everyone else had something different. When the check came and the money was collected, we were fifty-six dollars short. There was a fuss and a lot of recounting, but Mrs. Richest Woman at the Table held her ground and never owned up. Her friend put in the money for her because she felt sorry for this woman, whose husband was never home anymore.

I like classes, so I take a lot of them. Every time I take a class, it's as if I expect to find the answer I have missed along the way. But what I have missed along the way, I have found, is only what I have missed along the way. It isn't the answer. I know that now, but there was a time when you couldn't mention a subject without my saying, "I took a class in that." From celestial navigation to weight lifting, go through the alphabet—I took a class in it.

In LA, I took a screenwriting class that producers also attended in order to learn how to receive a writer's pitch. I learned there that most people write in teams. It's too lonely pasting index cards on the wall according to a prescribed formula, writing it all up by yourself, and in the end having the whole thing rewritten by strangers. Cartoon drawing, a Los Angeles City College adult extension course, was fun except that the students quickly became a group of extremely competitive six-year-olds trying to be proclaimed the best by the teacher. I learned how to grow roses and create a Zen garden. I went to spiritual retreats and took a trip to Findhorn, a New Age community in Scotland where I discovered synchronicity and how old I had suddenly gotten.

I bought a house.

My Hollywood Bungalow

My home, my Hollywood bungalow on Gardner Street, sat a block and a half above Melrose Avenue, where I could walk to dinner at a variety of restaurants, shop for vintage clothes, and find organic groceries at Quinn's Market. I could go to Canter's for lox and blintzes and catch an old Charlie Chaplin silent movie on Fairfax Avenue. On La Cienega, there was a mall with the current film hits playing. I could run around the track at Fairfax High, and my anxiety would melt away. It was almost a neighborhood.

My house had four rooms: a living room with a gas fireplace, a party-size kitchen, and two tiny rooms for a bedroom and a den. In the backyard, I intended to put a volleyball and badminton court and maybe a lap pool running along the side of my postage-stamp-size property.

The first night there, I was sitting with my friend Ron out on the flagstone patio, which was just off the kitchen and trellised with jasmine. We were surveying my estate and sipping a California chablis. I had recovered from my buyer's remorse. I had just finished saying, "Look at that full moon. Life is good," when there was a scrabbling, scratching, sliding sound on the roof above and behind us. We looked up and saw, lit by the moon against the dark sky, what appeared to be a small dog. We got a quick glimpse, and it was gone.

"What the heck was that? What's a dog doing up there?" I said.

"It wasn't a dog. It was a rat," said Ron.

"C'mon, it was *huge*. It was a huge animal."

"It was a rat," said Ron. "They're very large out here. They live in the—"

"Stop it! You're scaring me. Why is it . . . on my *rooftop?*"

"Well," said Ron, "they live in the palm trees, and it's probably trying to get in or out of your attic."

"My *attic!* Why doesn't he live in the sewer?"

"There aren't any sewers in LA," he said.

"There aren't?"

"It only rains about six days a year out here. Hadn't you noticed?"

"No. Why is that?"

"Well, LA was originally a desert, so—"

"You mean a *rat* the size of a *dog* is living in my *attic?*"

"You can put wire mesh over that hole next to your rain gutter and see what happens."

"This is a nightmare!"

The next day, I had to replace the clay plumbing pipe from the thirties that ran all the way down to the street. It seemed to have crumbled overnight.

Two weeks later, I came home in the middle of a burglary. The thieves were climbing out the back window as I turned the key in my front door. The curtain was still swaying in the breeze of their exit when I entered, and the stereo was gone. The next day, I put up window bars and a gate that locked across the driveway.

Nevertheless, I had some great parties there in that little house. All my guests liked all my other guests, much to their surprise. I also had house guests from New York and discovered that although it was great to have the company, I really preferred privacy at this time in my life. However, the time came when I was again faced with the loneliness and unreality of LA and the blanket of fear that lies over a company town.

One day I found that I didn't want to get rid of the ant that had gotten into my kitchen. That's how lonely it felt. I let him stay on as a pet. One night I spent an hour listening through thin walls to a rat crash and thrash around in a trap over my head before he gave up the ghost. I had the insane thought that I might miss him.

There was an old couple, Holocaust survivors, living next door to me who walked by my house every day on their way to lunch at a social center on Melrose. When the husband died, the wife would go alone and would stop and tell me sometimes how deeply she mourned him. About three months had gone by when I saw her walking home arm in arm with a new old fellow. She had met him at the social center, and pretty soon he moved in with her. She told me it wasn't that she didn't love her husband. She still loved him as deeply as she always had. "But, Peggy," she said, "I have to have a man in my bed."

Argyle Avenue

Thrusting up from downtown LA to the San Fernando Valley, the Hollywood Freeway soars over Sunset Boulevard, leaving an off-ramp to Argyle Avenue in its wake. Argyle Avenue is a wide street with white, wooden houses hugging the hill on each side of it along its first two blocks. The houses are made up of apartments. Farther up, set back and hidden behind greenery on the second block on the left, is a Russian mosque with an all-Russian-speaking congregation. A free Russian brunch is served after services on Sundays.

At the end of the second block, a mansion loafs across the avenue, forcing a right-angle turn into an abruptly narrowed street, joining the winding roads zigzagging through the Hollywood Hills and getting lost on Mulholland Drive, which winds west to the Pacific Ocean. Argyle Avenue is like a map of a Hollywood career that starts out with a flare and goes nowhere.

In the twenties and thirties, that mansion that dominates and shrinks the beginning of Argyle Avenue was where Barbara Stanwyck, Hedy Lamarr, Ginger Rogers, Olivia de Havilland, Veronica Lake, Jean Harlow, Greta Garbo, Joan Crawford, and Bette Davis lived together and entertained their gentlemen callers. Well, that was the *idea*, the fantasy. It was a new twist on an old business based on a fascination with the glamorous movie stars of the Hollywood studio system.

These women were look-alikes. There was a living, breathing, Madame Tussaud-seeming house of them. A movie star look-alike living and working there was required to do daily research on the star she was impersonating. By reading about her every day in the newspapers, gossip columns, and the trades, she found out what happened on the set where the star was working, what was said there, what parties the star went to, with whom she attended them, and what she wore.

If, say, Bette Davis were sick or away on location, her look-alike stayed in her room and didn't receive clients until Bette was back in town again.

I found Argyle Avenue one day while looking for yet another place to live. I had moved many times during my stay in Hollywood. I couldn't settle anywhere, but this street attracted me, invited me, said, "Oh, come live here, you'll love it." How quaint it was, off-beat, quiet, and peaceful. I moved into a complex of apartments that shared a wrap-around terrace filled with huge pots of red geraniums. Other actors—Dennis Christopher, Peter Frechette, and a costume designer for *Miami Vice*—were living there. I thought, *What a find, this charming "compound."* It was a modest rent, and we all had a second-floor bedroom and a garage underneath us. The Russian mosque hidden in the trees was just across the street.

It was a Wednesday. When I moved in on the following Saturday, I was shocked to find the street filled with cars, boom boxes, and Mexicans. I thought, *Gee, maybe it's a party.* But it was a party that happened every night. On weekends, cars were parked bumper to bumper along the sidewalks. During the day, rows of legs stuck out from under these cars as their owners worked on them with heavy wrenches that doubled as hammers. All this was accompanied by mariachis playing at top volume on the radio right under my living room window. They seemed to be in the room with me, and it wasn't long before I discovered that if I went out and asked them to be quiet, to go do their work somewhere else, they ignored me. This drove me nuts. I had moved into a ghetto, and nobody had warned me. I felt trapped, betrayed. The sun glared down as if to split my skin in two. I was coming apart; I was beside myself. There was impotence in my fury, and I screamed. I screamed at the Mexican who sat in his truck gunning his motor and drinking beer in front of my window. He never looked at me. I didn't exist for him. I was invisible to this profile of indifference in a pickup truck, this dark shadow of an archetype, this animus.

"Do you have a green card?" I heard myself shrieking.

Without a glance at me, he stripped into gear and drove away. I never saw him again.

My friend Brett said later, "You know, deep down everybody's a bigot when they're angry."

Next, I began to see hypodermic needles in the street. A couple of times, there was a shell casing in the gutter. Now and then there would be a muffled gunshot sound from deep inside the building directly across from me, where a shiny black car had pulled up briefly. Finally, one day around two o'clock in the afternoon, there was a loud, rapid knocking on my door and a voice crying, "Help! Help me! Please help me! He's beating me. He has a knife! I need help!"

I looked out the window and saw a scrawny girl in her late teens or early twenties, sobbing and pounding on my door. Since I didn't see anyone chasing her, I opened the door and said, "What's the matter? What is it? I'll call the police."

"No. No! No, please, miss. It's my boyfriend. He's after me. Please, no police!"

"Well, come in," I said. "What is it? Where is he?"

"I got away from him! He was beating me but I got away from him! He's chasing me . . . help me!"

"Come in," I said. She came in and stood on the threshold, sobbing and trembling.

"No, miss. Please. Thank you. No." She dissolved into a spasm of tears.

"Look," I said, "you need help. I'm going to find it for you. I'm going to look in the phone book and find a halfway house, a place where you can go where they know what to do for you."

"Thank you, missus," she said. I turned to get the phone book out and started to leaf through it. Something made me turn back to her, and I noticed that my wallet was on the floor. It had been sitting on the hall table next to my keys, and now it was on the floor. Leaning down to pick it up, I found it was empty. When I started to speak to the girl, I realized that she was gone. In the fraction of a second, she was gone. I couldn't believe it. It was like a bad script. I went out on the terrace to look for her, but she was gone, down the stairs, swallowed up by Argyle Avenue, over like a view out of a train window as one leaves the station, part of the past, no rewrites accepted.

Sometime later, after I had gotten away from there, I heard that the woman with the fine white hair and dirndl skirts who lived down the street from me went out with a camera when the shiny black car was visiting the druggies' house. As the driver was coming out, she said to him, "I just love your car. It is the most beautiful one of its kind I've ever seen. Cars are my hobby, you know. I'm a regular aficionado. You don't mind if I just take a little picture of it, do you?" She quickly snapped a picture of the car, including its license plate. "Thank you so much," she said over her shoulder as the driver said, "Wha——?" "And please give my regards to Mr.——" She mumbled some gibberish that was indistinguishable as she was halfway down the hill by then and had just about disappeared. Argyle Avenue never saw the car after that. I applaud that woman for her ingenuity, courage, and impeccable manners.

My last move was into a high-rise security condo on a different hill. Shortly thereafter, I went back to New York where the insanity was more familiar, allowing me to function in it at a higher level. In New York, I can stay in the same apartment for twenty years before I get the urge to move.

George Clooney and . . .

I was driving down Argyle Avenue on my way to the studio. As I crossed Hollywood Boulevard on a green light, a jalopy, barreling backward through the intersection, crashed into me. The driver got out. I knew her; she was an actress. The first thing she said was, "Where the hell is the Pantages Theatre?" I'm a good driver from the East, and I wasn't used to the insanity of this reaction I didn't tell her the Pantages was right behind her. I hope she's still looking for it.

When I got to makeup, George Clooney was standing there waiting his turn.

That's when I started to react to the accident. Delayed, hysterical sobs burst out of me. He stood there and listened. He was a wonderful listener. I had never been listened to so well in my life. I carried on a little longer than I needed to as a result.

Then we got to talking. He has a beautiful voice, although you can hardly hear it in his films. I asked him if he sang, too, like his aunt Rosemary, who was a favorite of mine. He said, "Nah, I gave it a shot, but I decided one singer in the family was enough."

He had come in late as a replacement on a TV pilot in which I played his mother. He did a scene in a real kitchen, where he cooked breakfast while he got dressed for work. He went from pajamas to business clothes, including tie, jacket, shoes, and socks, as he scrambled eggs, fried bacon, flipped pancakes, buttered toast, spread marmalade, and made coffee, which he drank. He had a bunch of lines that he knew perfectly, got all the jokes, and charmed us to pieces. He accomplished all of this in one take. There was a "Wow, how did you do that?" reaction from all of us and a great deal of applause.

Then the director said, "George, the scene can't go longer than four minutes. Could you cut twenty seconds off what you just did?"

George said, "Sure, why not?"

The next time I saw him was on the TV show *Sisters* in a scene with Sela Ward. I got to watch George keep the scene alive through sheer good nature and a sense of fun during the endless takes the cameras required. He never stopped. Between scenes he kept entertaining us.

I didn't have a scene with him on *ER* (I was playing a crazy lady whose husband had brought her in for a psychiatric evaluation because she'd freaked out over the rash of muggings in town), but George was right there making me, the new kid on the block, feel comfortable. He came over as soon as he saw me to find out if I needed anything. I showed him the seven guns my character had in her purse for protection and how I had learned to spin one of them around on my forefinger. He made a genuine effort to be impressed, but I could tell he had something else on his mind.

Another time I was eating lunch at the Farmers Market, a huge open-air restaurant in Hollywood, and George got up from his table on the other side of the patio where he was eating with a friend and came loping over. "How are you, Peggy? Everything all right?" He really wanted to know.

When I saw him in *Michael Clayton*, I realized in the middle of the picture that I had absolutely no idea where they were, who anybody was, or what was going on. Spy stories often do that to me. I had an impulse to leave, but then I thought, *No, I'm happy just sitting here watching him. I don't have to know anything past that.*

During the credits, he sits in the limo, thinking. That's it. I felt like I could read his mind by just watching his eyes. It was as if he were going over what had happened to him that day. It goes on for several minutes. I've never seen anything that simple and that riveting.

He talked about that moment in the profile *The New Yorker* did of him. In it, he said that what I saw was exactly what he had planned to do, think about the day. But a crowd had gathered to watch, and it struck him as so funny that all his thoughts and energy went into not cracking up. I saw his original intention for the scene anyway. It's a wonderful glimpse into the craft of acting, what the mind can juggle, and what a good actor he is.

Steve Guttenberg was another actor who was given me as a son in a TV pilot. I think it was only his second job. He was nineteen or twenty, and one day the soundstage got so frantic and out of control, with actors trying to shoot scenes while carpenters were still building the sets, that no one could remember any lines at all. It was Steve who showed me where to go for some quiet so I could learn lines while the set was exploding. He had found a hiding place and shared it with me. When I thanked him and told him what a great son he was, he said his mother had brought him up that way. Then he confided to me that once when he hadn't behaved well, she locked him out of the house in the middle of winter, and he didn't have any clothes on at all. But she wouldn't let him back in for half an hour, which he thanked her for to that day.

There was Jim Carrey, whom I never met but who walked through my kitchen in *Once Bitten*. I didn't know who he was at the time or I would have said, "Hello, son," and maybe reminded him to drink some orange juice.

And there was Mr. T from *The A—Team,* who told me that I reminded him of his mother. So I told him his shoes were a disgrace and that he should get a new pair. He had on the oldest, dirtiest, sloppiest pair of sneakers I'd ever seen. They were coming open at every seam. He said, "I'll never get rid of these shoes. They remind me of what I came from, and they'll keep me from getting a swelled head, 'cause if I don't pay attention, I'll end up right back there."

This was in Chicago, on the set of *The Toughest Man in the World*, a Movie of the Week about Mr. T's life. It was in his contract to be filmed where he came from so all the buddies he grew up with could be in the movie with him. It was a very unusual request, but it was granted.

Jane Fonda, after one of her scenes in *Nine to Five,* ended up sitting at the desk behind me and then was trapped there for the rest of the day in the background which had to be matched to the next scene, which was probably going to take all afternoon.

She said to me, "This is kind of a new experience for me, to sit here and be an extra in the scene. It feels really kind of boring." I said, "It is boring." I did it all the time. It's really only fun being in a film if you're in the whole thing or most of it, or if they film every scene you're in all on the same day or days. When they don't, which is pretty much always, you wait around all day and nearly go insane with boredom and anxiety, trying to keep your energy up and stay ready to say the lines they gave you at any moment. It's really deadly.

Jane Fonda had never been in that position. I don't know what she was experiencing, but she didn't seem to like my saying, in effect, that I was bored being in this film she was starring in. I was flat-out tactless in those days. I could have been warmer to her in her dilemma, but perhaps playing a drunk twelve hours a day for six weeks was making me cranky. I was sorry I had said what I did. I didn't see her after lunch that day. I think she spoke to someone and got excused.

Lily Tomlin came up to me the first day I was there and said, "I want to give you something. What could I bring on the set to give you?" I didn't know what she was talking about as we didn't really have a scene together, except for my saying, "Atta girl!" to her when she got pissed off at the boss. It was strange, but it was very generous. Later, I realized she was trying to make something of my presence on the set, to use everything around her. She surprised me. I had been thinking of the times our paths had crossed in a long hallway at a singing teacher's studio in the Ansonia Hotel, and how I had gone to see her one-woman show when she first started out. It was at the Playboy Club in New York. She opened as a woman networking at a funeral, waving, carrying on, chatting away, but it wasn't really Playboy material. I had been concerned about what might become of her.

Dame Judith

I got a call to be on *Santa Barbara,* the nighttime TV soap opera. I didn't have to read for it, which was unusual; I was just told to show up. The director greeted me cordially as soon as I was ushered onto the set.

"Dody," he said, "so glad you could join us."

He thought I was Dody Goodman, which happened a lot at the time. She was very hot on the nighttime talk shows at that time. I knew she'd broken her leg the day before, and some inspired casting director had sent me instead at the last minute, hoping to get away with it.

When I broke the news to the director, he was disappointed. He couldn't cover it up. It was not an encouraging moment for me, but I said I would do my best. The whole episode was soon overshadowed by the main event: Dame Judith Anderson, at the age of ninety-one, was to be on the show that day in a recurring part. We were told she would come in a limousine and go directly to makeup and wardrobe. When she was dressed and ready, no matter what they were shooting, everything would stop and they would do her scene. You don't keep a dame waiting.

When she arrived in the makeup room, I was there. Still in awe from having seen her Medea, I bided my time until she was alone, settled in a chair and waiting patiently to be made up, before I went over and greeted her. She was very gracious. I said, "I saw you in *Medea.*" Suddenly, she looked frightened. I had done that terrible thing, the unforgivable——I had told her I had seen her, never thinking to follow it up with how fabulous she was. It was a cardinal sin. How many times have people just said to me, "I saw you in the play," "I saw you on TV," or "I saw you in *Nine to Five.*" Once a woman in an elevator said to me with a touch of annoyance, "I saw you on my TV *again* last night," as if I had deliberately and personally taken over her living room and it was getting on her nerves. However they're delivered, these remarks can invoke the impulse to reply, "Well, how was I?" You can't help it. With Judith Anderson, I assumed she knew she was magnificent and that I really didn't need to tell her so. Realizing my faux pas, I tried to recover. I gushed. I told her about having the catharsis I had never experienced in college. I carried on until it was embarrassing, but she looked relieved.

"Oh, good," she said. "I was worried there for a minute that perhaps you hadn't liked me." She changed the subject immediately to Robinson Jeffers and how it was he, with his adaptation, who had been the center of the production. The thought went through my mind, *Does it never end for an actor? Does one always wonder if one is good enough?*

After she was dressed and ready, two escorts appeared with a vodka cocktail, which she sipped. Then they walked her to the set. All other action stopped as she made her way to her place. She did her scene, and when she came back, she was presented with the rest of the cocktail, which she downed immediately. She got into her street clothes and then into her waiting limo and was driven home to Montecito. She didn't live in Hollywood.

For me, this was a piece of history. I was sorry Dody Goodman had had to miss it.

BACK HOME

There's an actor's story about how time expands as it's contracting in LA. I think Hilda Haynes told it first. It goes like this: You get up in the morning, go out to the pool, have some breakfast, read the trades, go for a swim, come back inside, and find you are eighty-two years old.

After stretching my five-year "Improve My Career" plan in LA to fifteen years, I was about 107 and it was time to go back to New York. There, I was in eleventh heaven rehearsing Steve Martin's play *WASP,* live at the Public Theater. Steve was there every day with his laptop, rewriting, telling us we were wonderful, taking us to dinner, sitting in cabs with us, carrying his guidebook *Men Are from Mars, Women Are from Venus* with him. It was great.

Then one day the flu hit me. I had forgotten all about the flu. My fever climbed to 104 degrees, and I was barely able to stand. I tore myself away from my new best friends, boarded a crowded subway, and prayed I'd make it home.

When I got off at Seventy-Second Street, I headed for a bench in the station, thinking I'd just sit down and rest for a minute before attempting the stairs. *If I can just make it to the bench . . .* I felt dizzy. People pushed by me, but I kept focused on that bench, so solid, so secure, offering me such solace. Three or four feet away from it, in slow motion, I reached out for the wooden armrest and sank to my knees like an invalid at Lourdes. Then I put my head down, laid my cheek on the platform, and thought, *Oh, I'll just take a little nap right here.* I tried to raise my head and fainted.

When I came to, there was nobody around. Something was wrong. The Broadway and 72ndStreet subway station empty? Then I saw him about ten feet away, watching me. He was wearing baggy brown trousers, a beat-up corduroy jacket he might have slept in, a cap on his head, his hands in his pockets, a potbelly for a stomach.

"Oh. What happened?" I said.

"Ya passed out. Ha ha." He looked like a guy who might hang out at the Off Track Betting Booth. He hitched up his trousers, shifting his "equipment" from left to right and back again. He made me nervous.

"How long have I been like this?" I asked.

"Four, five minutes," he said.

"You clocked it?" I asked.

Was there no one else around? How was I going to get away from this crazy?

No part of my body was working. Was this how it was all going to end? Could I not even whimper?

He didn't move either. He studied me like I was a chess game. He said, "Haven't I seen you on TV?"

"Would you please help me up?" I said. "Help me up! Up!"

"Sure, sure," he said. He came over and extended a hand, and then, like a little child asking if there really is a Santa Claus, he asked, "What's Dolly Parton really like?"

A Recipe

Around the corner from where I live in New York is a Greek restaurant called Nick's. It's very good. It has Christmas lights up year-round and tables on the sidewalk. Greek music plays constantly. A slide show of the Greek Islands dances on the walls.

If you've been to Greece, Nick's will bring up memories for you as it does for me: hiking up to the Parthenon to see the Vestal Virgins losing themselves in their Dionysian dance, wanting to join them; tracing Lord Byron's signature on the front of the temple at Cape Sunion; spending the rest of the day gazing at the Aegean Sea, the sky so luminous a blue that I never wanted to leave; looking down from the top of Mykonos at a lone sailboat, lazily anchored in a tiny harbor; taking a small boat the next day to the deserted island of Apollo, the god of love, to see the giant stone penises dedicated to him; looking up at the shepherds' mountain caves on Crete where the hippies lived after WWII; and wandering through the palace where Theseus slew the Minotaur. Ah, here's the waiter. Time to order.

I'm looking at desserts. Here's one, kataifi. It made me think of Dolly Parton: rich, light, sweet, served hot or cold. I had been wanting to ask her if she would give me a recipe for this book, just for fun, since *Nine to Five,* to many people, is who I am. I don't need to bother her now. She could be writing a song. I got this recipe from Nick.

Kataifi
Walnuts, almonds, honey, shredded filo dough, and syrup
Served warm $6.95   A la mode $7.50
If you have a leftover drink, like Campari and orange juice, just add it in.

I had mine warm.

Good-Bye, Dolly

Dolly Parton was a glowing presence on the set. She was quiet and friendly. You could talk to her easily—though briefly. She would come through the door to the soundstage and pass the catering table where there was always a stagehand or two loitering, waiting to get a breath of her to go with his coffee. She would smile generously as she passed by. Maybe she'd say, "Mmmm, what have they got today? Ooh, donuts," and never stop walking.

Each time her work on the set was done, she'd head back out to her dressing room/trailer by the same route, leaving stardust and lust in her wake. Between scenes, she wrote songs, planned Dollywood, and worked on her franchises, so she didn't have time to schmooze.

I never had a full conversation with her. I had a moment, a line in the scene when she storms out of the boss's office, where he'd been harassing her. She announces she's going out to get a drink, at which point I say, "Atta girl!" to her. She was wonderful and never seemed to need direction or many takes. It was all business, like working in an office for real.

About six weeks after *Nine to Five* wrapped, I went to the theater and saw her across the auditorium. She saw me and screamed with delight, "Peggy!" She ran over to me on her high heels and gave me a huge hug. The heat coming out of her was so intense that it was like being embraced by the sun.

And I never saw her again. Showbiz.

A Crowded Elevator

Jammed up against me in a crowded elevator, a stranger, his lips barely moving, said quietly, "Over the years, you've made me laugh." That was it. That was the best. I never saw him again, either.

Afterword

Ice

I'm retired now. I live on a lake and go skate-sailing in the winter, by the light of the moon. Out there I fly faster than I want, but I keep going. The crossbar of the sail rests on my shoulder, a plastic window allows me a blurred view. Blown by the fierce wind, I leave a trail of parallel white lines on the black ice. The cold pierces my bones, my blood, my soul; it's a cold whirling in a wind that would freeze my eyeballs. But I'm wearing goggles.

Black ice, smooth as glass, frozen suddenly when there was no wind to ripple across it and turn it white. Solid cold, straight down to the bottom of the lake. I can see through the blackness suspended under my skates, a still life of branches, beer cans, plastic bags, a picnic basket, a rubber tire, a sled, a bicycle, a car hood, maybe twenty-five condoms and what looks like a toupee, some liposuction leftovers, and part of a hand, all the way down to the background of black mud.

In the distance, the ghost of my father, costumed as Tiresias, that grumpy old guy, that blind, scraggly prophet, hobbles by on his double runners with a sandwich board that says, "Greet Your Last Dog-Eat-Dog Day." That's all right. He's come through before. Soon it will be spring and then summer, and then, God willing, we can all go swimming again.

Fin